No Ordinary Days

SUSAN SYGALL

With

Ken Spillman

No Ordinary Days

Published by Outer Hebrides Press, Eugene, Oregon
Cover design by Chris Berner
Back cover photograph by Thomas Boyd
ISBN: 978-0692253458
First printing, 2014
Printed in the United States of America

In loving memory of my parents,

Mike and Lisa Sygall

לְמְנוֹת יָמֵינוּ כֵּן הוֹדַע   וְנָבִיא לְבַב חָכְמָה:

Teach us to treasure each day.
That we may open our hearts to Your Wisdom,
Teach us to treasure each day.

Translation: Rabbi Yitzhak Husbands-Hankin

ACKNOWLEDGEMENTS

It would be impossible to read this book without realizing that I am fortunate to have many wonderful friends and colleagues. Without such people, *No Ordinary Days* simply could not have been written.

At the outset, I acknowledge the many other disability rights activists around the world and especially my mentors, Pat Wright, Mary Lou Breslin and Ralf Hotchkiss. I honor Patty Overland and Corbett O'Toole, who were pioneers in creating disabled women's culture and pride. I thank the many people who assisted in the establishment of the Berkeley Outreach Recreation Program (BORP) and Mobility International USA (MIUSA), and made them the nationally recognized programs they are today. A special thanks to Linda Phelps for her dedication to the formation and success of MIUSA over many, many years. I also wish to acknowledge the resilient and inspirational women who have participated in MIUSA's International Women's Institutes on Leadership and Disability (WILD).

My colleague and friend Cerise Roth-Vinson taught me – in her fun-filled, non judgmental way – how to manipulate the technology necessary to create a book; while Cindy Lewis, my soul sister, assisted me enormously with the early stages of the book. Rich Glauber met me numerous times in a café to help me shape the book proposal, while Dr. Binh in Vietnam kept me accountable with his short but poignant emails: "How is your book, Susan?"

I extend my love and thanks to Dr. Gene Bolles and also want to acknowledge my dear friends Evelyn Anderton, Trevor Bailey, Patti and Tom Barkin, Sandra Birnbaum, Suzan Dawe, Dr. Deborah Dotters, Susan Dunn, Jane Falls, Dolfy Freinquel, Joanne and Marv Granek, Mark Hansen, Rod Hart, David Helfand, Shonna Husbands-Hankin, Lise Jaffe, Gary Johnson, Essam Kamal, Mark Kapelushnik, Linda Kessel, Dr. Christine Kollmorgon, Enid Lefton, Cynthia Lewis-Berry, Dr. Martha MacRitchie, Bernie Maengen, Jerry Pergamit, Linda Phelps, Adrian Quevado, Heshy Rabinowitz, Joyce Rosenbaum, Debbie Schechter, Diane Schechter, Sally Sheklow, Lydia Shula, Dr. Jenny Soyke, Robin Wells, Barbara Williams-Sheng, Rabbi Yitzchak Husbands-Hankin, Barbara Yost, and Randy Zeidberg. I would like to especially acknowledge Emily Heilbrun for her friendship and endless dedication to this endeavor. In addition, I'm eternally grateful to Peter DeFazio, Bob Persiko, David Levin, Greg Dixon, the Kellogg Foundation, Rotary International and the MacArthur Foundation for believing in me and supporting my goals, especially when they were no more than untested ideas.

Without my co-writer Ken Spillman, this book would not have come to fruition. Perhaps the story of Ken's involvement in this book is as powerful as anything that is included in my memoir. We met in 1979, when I attended the University of Queensland in Australia. He was a lean young man of twenty – reserved, thoughtful and unlike any of the other "blokes." I was impressed by his insights, and by his poetry. I located Ken on the internet at a time when I was discouraged by the publishing world and ready to abandon the idea of writing a book. By then he was an established author, and he strongly encouraged me to write my memoir, unselfishly offering to edit and shape the book as I went along. Over the ensuing years we emailed back and forth and Ken became my closest friend, helping me weather the darkest storms of my life. What amazes me most is that this was all done via email, and I will treasure the moment when we celebrate the book together, more than three decades after we first met.

Finally, heartfelt thanks to Tom Broeker, my life partner. Tom encouraged me and listened to my excitement and my frustrations, never wavering in his certainty that this book was important and needed to be published. His love and faith in my goals, and in me, have been a constant in a life of many unexpected turns.

Susan Sygall

No Ordinary Days

1.

At the rehab center in the middle of Manhattan, the halls were gray. Everything was gray. People would hang around in wheelchairs, some waiting for therapy sessions and some waiting for someone to give them a push. Some, I think, were waiting for another life.

Another life

It was a clear day, with clear skies over the campus of the University of Colorado. Boulder is a beautiful college town set against the spectacular backdrop of the Rocky Mountains. Jagged peaks pierce the cloudless blue sky.

I had climbed those mountains, with my strong legs and new hiking boots. I had climbed those mountains with a beautiful, red-haired boy who was passing through Colorado and wanted to "crash" in the room I shared with a fellow student, Elaine. The boy's name was Matt. He came into my life for a few days and then continued on his travels. I liked the way he smelled as we climbed the rocks. It was a soft, sweet smell, and his smile was sweet and gentle too. He was about six feet tall and very fit, like me. We kept a good pace and spoke sparingly, enjoying the brisk air and the occasional song of a bird.

The details of this day would never be forgotten.

In front of our dormitory under that perfect blue sky, I threw a Frisbee with Elaine. A geology major, Elaine had also spent many days climbing and exploring the Rockies. We laughed as we ran and jumped to catch our Frisbee, over and over again. We fell to the ground laughing. I was wearing a headscarf—a first for me—and the braces were just off my teeth. It was nearing the end of the summer session and I was happy. I was taking courses in modern dance, philosophy and therapeutic recreation. I was enveloped by blue skies and limitless possibility.

This was a day that spanned two lives.

It was a pivotal day when one life ended and another began. I would need to start again, carrying the memory of strong legs, dexterity and ease. These would be precious memories, forever in my consciousness.

I would still feel the exhilaration of conquering obstacles and climbing mountains—but in a very different way.

29 August 1971

In my therapeutic recreation class, the professor asked whether any of us had heard of wheelchair basketball. I hadn't, and I wasn't alone. The professor explained how disabled Vietnam War veterans—the paralyzed and amputees—were learning this game. He said that, as recreational therapists, we would need to get into a wheelchair, play the game, and help those disabled men adjust to their new life.

I raised my hand. "I don't think I could do that", I told him. "I have been athletic all my life and couldn't imagine playing basketball in a wheelchair."

What I didn't say was that I wouldn't *want* to do that, and couldn't imagine why they would either. The next day, I was going to be trying out for the University of Colorado women's basketball team.

Or so I thought.

29 August 1971.

A perfect day.

Or so it seemed.

After playing Frisbee with Elaine, I showered ready to meet Faisal in the evening. Faisal and I were co-captains of the intramural volleyball team, and I was very much attracted to him. He came from Kuwait, and was forbidden fruit. I am Jewish, and loved comparing his Arabic with the Hebrew I had learned. I also loved hearing stories about Faisal's home country. I was on a mission, proving that Arabs and Jews didn't need to hate each other. Faisal said he wanted me to visit Kuwait some day.

We had arranged to meet after I went along to hear a famous guru speak on campus. I was curious about this guru and wanted to see why he had such a following, but after a while I decided it wasn't my kind of thing. I left early, met Faisal, and we decided to drive to the top of Flagstaff, the lookout point at the top of a mountain crest. I wasn't planning to stay out late because of the basketball trials the next day.

I got into Faisal's Mustang. I put on my seatbelt and we drove for a while. We stopped halfway up the mountain to look at the breathtaking views, throwing pebbles into pools of water by the road. Then we got back into the car and drove to the top. Faisal had been at a party and, standing close to him, I noticed the smell of liquor on his breath. He tried to kiss and make out, but I wanted to get back to the dorm. The basketball trials were important to me and I needed sleep. That annoyed him.

We started down the mountain, the road looping and twisting like the coils of a spring. Faisal drove fast. I sat tight, leaning this way and that like a downhill skier.

"Slow down."

He ignored me.

"Slow down."

The Mustang's tires screeched on another bend.

"Slow down!"

Still he didn't listen. The car began to skid on a turn. It revolved almost 360 degrees and hurtled toward a wall of rock. At almost fifty miles per hour we slammed into it, passenger side first.

There was the sound of a glass shower, like light rain.

Everything switched to slow motion. I saw things clearly, heard things acutely. Feelings registered slowly. A tingling sensation started somewhere above my hips and trickled into my legs like pins and needles.

Then nothing — there was no feeling below my waist.

Nothing.

I couldn't move.

At all.

I knew — with absolute certainty — that my life had changed forever.

Perfect imperfect

My mother had another seizure just a few hours before the Passover *seder*. I was out when I got the call, but arrived a few minutes later. She was pale, clammy, semi-conscious. Her skin was moist and yellowy-green.

Seizures had become regular occurrences. I'd kiss her soft, warm skin and hold her hand as she drifted into a euphoric, post-seizure sleep. I would think about the mom she was when I was little. We had reversed roles at some point, and it wasn't always easy to remember when things were different.

My room in New York was small and pink. There were pictures of ballerinas on the wall. The floor was bright pink linoleum with Humpty Dumptys and other nursery rhyme characters dancing around. There were many dolls, large and small, and lots of stuffed animals because my father worked in a Brooklyn doll factory and brought home samples. My mom was an ice skating teacher, the director of a school with hundreds of students, some perhaps dreaming of becoming Olympians.

We lived in a modest, middle-floor apartment. My parents were Holocaust survivors who immigrated to the United States after World War II. If there were a book titled *The Daughter Who Loved her Parents Too Much*, I would be the author.

They deserved that—it went both ways. I received unconditional love from two people who enjoyed every minute of life and never worried about small things. They had a sense of perspective. When I got a bad grade in math they said not to worry.

"Maybe the teacher isn't so good," they would say.

If I spilled milk all over the table, we laughed. "Don't

worry — it's nothing."

When I wanted to drink my chocolate milk from a bowl and pretend I was a dog, my mother said it was fine.

I was loved and cared for by people full of love and caring. They savored everyday experiences — a beautiful sky, the smell of fresh coffee, a good prune Danish, chocolate cake for breakfast.

Like my mom, I was athletic and learned sporting skills easily. I was smart in school and did well in languages — it probably helped that my dad spoke more than eight languages, which he learned during fifteen years at sea.

I learned a lot about values. My parents didn't buy much, only things we really needed. Instead, they spent their hard-earned money on traveling, and I went with them on vacations to Florida, Colombia and faraway islands.

When I was nine, I began spending summers at Jewish camps in New Hampshire. I had lots of friends and loved being out in the open air, suffused with the heady smell of pine trees. We spent our days playing sports and singing Hebrew songs. I was happy. But I always cried before I left my parents. Somewhere deep inside, I was afraid that I might never see them again.

I cried when I was nine. I cried when I went off to college. I cried when I left for Australia for postgraduate study.

Can a daughter love her parents too much?

Did being the daughter of parents whose family members were murdered in the Holocaust create an exceptionally strong bond, connecting me to the souls of relatives never met?

One day, near the ocean on a vacation, my mom and dad tried talking to me about the arrangements that should be made when they died. I became hysterical, bursting into tears the way I did when I said goodbye.

"But Susan," they said, holding me. "We all must die, sooner or later."

I didn't want to hear it.

Can a daughter love her parents too much?

No. But I feel my parents inside of me. When I spill milk on the table, see a beautiful sky, eat chocolate cake for breakfast.

I'm happy with an imperfect world.

I'm perfect just the way I am.

Imperfect.

Expect the worst, hope for the best

Faisal lifted me out of the car and laid me on the ground next to it. I told him to get help, to find someone who could get an ambulance. Soon there were voices. People were stopping their cars. They were thinking about trouble, about blame.

"Be sure you don't have any drugs in the car, man..."

All I wanted was for Faisal to send these people to call for an ambulance. I was repeating myself, pleading. I had no scratches, no scrapes, no bleeding—but I was paralyzed from the waist down.

Finally I heard a siren. The medics moved me onto a stretcher and slid it into the ambulance. We sped away, siren blaring again.

I was conscious.

Super conscious.

In the emergency room, a kind young doctor with blue green eyes and a smooth, clean-shaven face took my hand.

"Am I going to die?"

"We have to do surgery," he said. "And there is always a chance you can die during surgery."

"Will I be able to walk again?"

"I don't know," he replied. "Expect the worst, hope for the best."

Expect the worst, hope for the best. Those words, little sound waves, struck my eardrums and reverberated throughout my being.

"I need to call your parents."

"Oh no, you can't do that! They'll kill me," I replied.

I was imagining the horror my parents would feel at the news that their daughter was in an accident with a Muslim man from Kuwait.

But I had no choice. I gave the doctor my parents' phone number in New York. He took my hand and I was wheeled into an operating room. White lights glared from the ceiling. A team of people wearing surgical green and latex gloves looked down at me.

"Good luck," I told them.

They placed something over my mouth and nose.

Finally, I lost consciousness.

The phone call

I don't know what happened after my parents got the call in the middle of the night. Sometime later, I think, I heard them talking about calling some friends and getting a ride to JFK airport for the next available flight to Denver.

I more clearly remember being told of their reaction when

they met the young neurosurgeon, Dr. Gene Bolles. Dr. Bolles told my parents gently, yet candidly, that he didn't know whether their daughter would ever walk again, and that he didn't even know how long she would need to spend in rehabilitation.

My mom asked him the questions she believed to be most important.

If her daughter wasn't able to walk again, could she have sex?

Could she have children?

My mom and dad were taken aback by the neurosurgeon's appearance. He was young, too young. He wore a plaid shirt and corduroy pants. Was this his first operation? How experienced was he? Should they get another opinion from an older, more experienced doctor from Denver?

I don't know what they asked Dr. Bolles about the man driving the car.

That topic was never discussed.

Never.

Faisal

Somewhere in my attic is a box of files.

The files contain legal documents, depositions, transcripts. If you were to open them up, you could read everything I said to the lawyers who came to see me after I was moved from Boulder to a rehab center in Manhattan.

You could also read what Faisal said.

Faisal only came to see me once at the hospital in Boulder. It was late at night after visiting hours. I thought he was there to comfort me, and to apologize. Instead, he said it wasn't his fault and that he didn't want to lose his University of Colorado scholarship.

Faisal was not injured in the car accident. I was paralyzed for life.

He never came to see me again.

He tried to sue me for the damage to his car.

Where is Faisal now? Is he a prince? A businessman? Does he ever think of what happened back then?

The lawyers told me that Faisal didn't care about me because I'm Jewish. I never tell anyone about him. His treatment of me has been my secret.

Sometimes I have wondered what I'd do if I saw Faisal. I know that every time I'm sitting in the passenger seat of a car, and we take a bend on a road, I hear my own voice.

"Slow down."

I grip the seat or the armrest and brace myself. In my mind, the car goes into a slide and I hit the Rocky Mountains all over again.

P-a-r-a-p-l-e-g-i-c

They prescribed anti-depressants so that I wouldn't get too upset about my predicament.

I did what I was told, took what I was given.

A day or so after regaining consciousness, I asked for the name of my condition.

"Would you mind spelling that?"

"P-a-r-a-p-l-e-g-i-c."

I was extremely happy. Almost ecstatic. I didn't know why.

I was eighteen and paralyzed for life. I couldn't move or feel anything below my waist. How could I be happy?

Finally I learned that it was because I'd been prescribed mood-altering drugs. I demanded to be taken off them immediately.

After a time, the psychologist came to visit me.

"I understand what you are going through. It's completely understandable that you are depressed. That's only natural. You'll never walk again. You must be so angry."

It was him I was angry with.

You're an idiot, I thought. Never walk again? Who says so? How would you know? A man who met me five minutes ago, some old guy – maybe nearly forty – walking around with a stupid little notebook. What could you know about me? There is no way I am never going to walk again. Don't you know that if I don't walk perfectly by next year, when my high school reunion takes place, I'll have to kill myself? You know nothing about the legs I can't feel, the catheter draining my urine. You know nothing about how I feel. How dare you presume that you might even have a clue?

"I never want him back in my room," I told the nurse after he left. "Never."

Many years later, I realized that this was the outburst of a highly traumatized teenager. But it wasn't that alone. Contained within it were some important insights, some truths.

Non-disabled people don't know what it's like to be disabled.

They don't know the good or the bad of it, and they never will. They shouldn't be expected to know, either. It's not their experience.

How dare they act as if it is?

I'll be there

Mark also got a phone call. I don't know who delivered the news. I do know that when he heard that I'd been in "a bad accident", he didn't ask any questions.

"I'll be there," he said.

I met Mark in summer camp when I sixteen. I remember wrestling with him on the lawn. I was tall and slim, and my fit legs gleamed in the sunlight of those summer days. I was an assistant counselor teaching archery, and he was a dishwasher who lived with the other kitchen help above the dining room. He was a lean boy, and a great dancer.

I loved to dance.

After knowing each other for about three days, we were going steady. I wore his ring, with the initials of his name, proudly dangling around my neck. To be honest, I didn't even know what his last name was — it was some sort of Polish name — but at sixteen those details seemed unimportant.

Mark was intense — quiet and deep like a mountain lake. His parents were Jewish immigrants from Europe, much like mine. He could get angry if I folded maps the wrong way on a road trip to the countryside, but he was fiercely loyal. Mark didn't talk a lot, but he meant every word he said.

He loved fishing, and being alone.

"We could get married and live in a cabin in the woods," he

would say. "That's all I need to make me happy."

After summer camp ended, he took the subway from the Bronx to Queens to visit me. We spent many hours doing everything — but not "it". We would sit on the couch in the living room after my parents went to sleep, pretending to watch television as we kissed and held each other. When I was eighteen, my mother suggested that I should see a doctor about birth control. It was good advice — probably, just in the nick of time.

Mark and I were great together, but I wanted to go beyond New York, while he needed to be at a school he could afford. He was at the University of Brockport in upstate New York, studying philosophy, when he got the call from Colorado.

"I'll be there."

He borrowed money from a friend and, the next day, boarded an airplane. He dropped out of Brockport and stayed with me for six weeks, getting a job in a nearby Baskin and Robbins ice cream store and bringing a different ice cream to my room every evening.

Mark knew that I loved his thick, wavy hair — but the owner of the ice cream store wanted a short-haired, clean-cut person. He had the perfect solution: he bought a wig that made it look like he had short hair.

"Anything for Susan."

I'd experienced life-changing trauma, but there wasn't any talk about breaking up, or about how things would change between us.

"We'll move to Nova Scotia," Mark said. He had lost his draft deferment for Vietnam, so Canada was an obvious choice.

"We'll buy a log cabin — doesn't matter if you walk again or not."

Dr. Bolles

Dr. Bolles took on extraordinary importance for me. When I was in pain, they paged him to change my medication. When he came to see me, he pricked me with a safety pin attached to his crisp, light blue shirt, checking whether I had regained any skin sensation in my legs or anywhere below my waist.

Most importantly, late at night when all the lights were off and I was alone in my room, I heard his gentle knock on my door. After he had finished his rounds of patients and completed all the necessary paperwork, he would stop by my room to ask how I was.

He would hold my hand. He would be honest. Expect the worst, hope for the best. I felt that he really cared about me.

As years passed, I would find out how much.

Believing

My parents remained their optimistic selves.

"We will make the best of it," my dad told me.

"Susan," my mom said, "I don't know how things will turn out, but it will be okay. We can get through this. We are strong."

They never said, "We have been through worse and have come out okay," but that thought lingered in the air, without need of expression.

I believed them.

I believed *in* them.

That is how we lived our lives — believing.

2.

At night I dreamed of running. I ran along sandy beaches with the ocean breeze in my hair. I ran through forests. I ran, ran, ran. The dreams occurred every night and I loved them. I woke refreshed. Their reality seemed more real than the gray walls of rehab.

Rehab

After six weeks at the hospital in Colorado, I was transferred by stretcher on an army medical evacuation plane to New York for rehab.

The Manhattan rehab centre was a place of gray halls and waiting. Everyone seemed to be waiting. There were people in beds, waiting. There were people in wheelchairs, waiting. Some were waiting for another life, but only a few would end up with one that resembled the life they were hoping for.

On my floor, most people were in their twenties or early thirties but, at eighteen, I was two years older than my roommate. Rehab is a time warp. Nothing seems real, which makes it easy to believe that it isn't really *you* in there. Can it really be *you* surrounded by people in wheelchairs?

It was.

It was me.

It was me lying flat on my back in a strange bed — a large, circular structure. Every two hours, they'd put another frame on top of me and rotate the bed. I was like the meat in a sandwich. Sometimes I'd face the ceiling, sometimes I faced the floor.

I was to stay like that for six months — never sitting up or even raising my head. I didn't have any tubes or medical gadgets attached to me because they were trying to see what level of normalcy my body would return to. I had pads stuffed under me to soak up my urine. I didn't have any control over that, and was at the mercy of aides who changed my pads, sheets and clothes. After being given laxatives every few nights, I would defecate on myself and again wait for someone to find the time to change me.

I figured out that it was best to have my TV set showing the aides' favorite televisions programs — soap operas like *All My Children*. That way, there was more of a chance that someone would come and help me.

Many years later, I found myself secretly turning on *All My Children* to catch up with the characters' lives. I also developed a very low tolerance to pee and poop. If I had an "accident" in my pants, which is not so uncommon after a spinal injury, I'd throw my underpants into the garbage. Too many bad memories. I just didn't want to have to deal with them.

Rehab days were filled with lying in bed, listening to music and having painful physical therapy to keep some range of motion in my legs. My parents visited me every night — my father came in after leaving work in Brooklyn, while my mom took the subway from Queens and then rode home with my dad.

Friends visited and I heard about lives that had not been

interrupted. They were playing sports, skiing, competing in gymnastics. When my brother visited, he tried to pick up my girlfriends. Why couldn't he leave them alone? They were the only friends I had, and it was another reminder that I was paralyzed in bed while everyone else went on with their lives.

Mark

My boyfriend Mark returned to New York when I was transferred, and he came to visit me every night. We made out. We did as much as it was possible to do with only a curtain concealing us from the three other people in my hospital room.

Insecurity visited when Mark left. I remembered hearing Mark say that he looked at other girls, that this was natural. I remembered how he said that he noticed their pretty hair, their eyes, or their attractiveness in some other way. At the time, I was horrified.

Back then, at sixteen or seventeen, I had imagined that being in love meant never noticing anyone else. In fairy tales, the hero never scooped up a young maiden and, while keeping her safe on his white stallion, looked over her shoulder to check out all the other maidens.

With my legs atrophying and with my lack of ability to use a toilet or a shower, it's no wonder I felt insecure.

Connected

From the rehab center, I wrote to Dr. Bolles thanking him, never expecting to hear back.

One day, after a particularly grueling physical therapy session, I was wheeled back to my room to find a letter from him. Dr. Bolles continued to write me throughout my stay in rehab.

Some years later, I went to visit him in Colorado. I was in my wheelchair, and it was the first time I'd seen him without being flat on a bed with his eyes looking down at me.

He was shorter than I imagined. We hugged, we embraced, we laughed. Maybe one of us cried a little.

We remained connected in a unique way.

We stayed in touch.

While I was a student at Berkeley, I had a complication and flew to Boulder to get his opinion. He took a loose wire from my back, one that he had placed there years earlier, and stitched me up. Afterwards, we went up to a restaurant in the Rocky Mountains and ate Steak Diane.

When I developed another complication, he flew at his own expense to Oregon, where I then lived, to assist with an operation to put a shunt into my back where a liquid cyst had developed. Before the operation, we went out to a jazz restaurant with my parents.

Later still, after my dad died, Dr. Bolles accompanied my mom and me on a visit to the White House where I got an award from President Bill Clinton. He also took me helicopter fishing in Alaska, flying over glaciers and landing in the wilderness where wild bears roamed.

No. Not your typical doctor-patient relationship, but one of the most important relationships of all.

This friendship shaped how I dealt with my injuries from the car accident.

It helped make me who I am today.

29 August 1971.

Not just another day for me, and not just another day at the hospital for him. I was never a nameless patient. My fate rested in his hands, and in his heart.

The philosophy of Bill

Bill was a quadriplegic whose room was down the hall from mine. He was in his early thirties, with a thin face, wire-rimmed glasses and brown curly hair. Using his electric wheelchair, he sometimes cruised down the hall to visit me.

Bill was a "high quad", which means that he broke his neck at a high cervical level and was paralyzed from the chest down, including his arms and fingers. His hands were in splints to give him more mobility, and he could only just manage to use the switch on his wheelchair.

Like all of us in rehab, Bill was newly injured. Like all of us, he moved through the gray halls wondering what the hell happened. Bill had been an artist, a sculptor living in Greenwich Village in New York City. He was starting to fulfill his dreams. Then he dived into shallow water and hit rock bottom.

How does a person deal with such trauma? What could he do now?

One day, Bill taught me a most important lesson. It wasn't a speech or a sermon—just a casual conversation in the hall. It changed my life.

I asked how he coped with what had happened to him. My real question was: how do *I* cope with what happened to *me*?

Bill told me what he imagined. He imagined that, at the moment he plunged into the water, his life ended. The memory of the life he'd had remained—painting and sculpting, late night parties, going for long walks—but it was only a memory.

It was a nice life, but it was gone.

Gone. That particular Bill was dead. Death happens.

Now there was a second life—in rehab, paralyzed, dealing with a divorce. There was no turning back, no comparing this life with the one he had before.

There were to be no regrets, no "what ifs".

That life is over. This life is here. They are separate.

Long afterward, after I got out of rehab, I tried to find Bill. I wanted to tell him that our short conversation in that ugly gray hall helped me—no, that it *saved* me. I found him in a small apartment in Manhattan. It was a wheelchair accessible place, a sterile apartment with wide doors and an elevator. It wasn't Greenwich Village, with artists hanging out and streets lined with cafés, curbs and obstructions.

Bill's apartment was messy and dark, filled with stale cigarette smoke. Bill seemed sad, but he was amused to see me after so many years.

I told him how much his words had meant to me. I recounted our conversation, told him that he gave me a philosophy that worked.

He didn't remember it.

Irreversible

When you're in rehab things can seem more than real, or they can seem less than real. You don't really confront reality until your first time outside the automatic doors. Then it hits you.

I was with Mark. We were heading toward 34th Street, packed with cars on a weekday morning. I had almost forgotten how it felt to be out in the fresh air. For the first time, I was out in the world in a wheelchair.

A wheelchair.

I was totally unprepared for it. People seemed to be staring at me. I was nineteen years-old and in a wheelchair, and I suddenly realized that it was not just *for now*. It was *for always*. This wasn't someone else's life. It was mine. I wasn't in Colorado with a scarf on my head throwing Frisbees. I wasn't running in the wind.

I was in a wheelchair in Manhattan, with a support brace on my back.

We went into a small, dim Irish restaurant to celebrate my first trip out.

The tears started to fall, and they didn't stop. I sobbed uncontrollably. I was ruining my first outing, but I couldn't help it.

For the first time since Faisal's Mustang hit the Rocky Mountains, I could fully comprehend what had happened.

It was irreversible.

P-a-r-a-p-l-e-g-i-c.

Surprise visitor

Almost a year after the accident, I was told that someone was waiting for me in the sunroom on the ground floor. I pushed my wheelchair into the elevator, knowing it couldn't be any of my regular visitors. I was curious about who this surprise visitor might be.

As I got closer, I recognized Matt, the red-haired backpacker from another life. He was holding a bottle of Italian wine — Bolla valpolicella, all the way from Veneto. I had no idea how Matt could have found out what happened to me, no idea how he had traced me to that strange, gray corner of New York.

At first I was self-conscious about being in a wheelchair with him, but he was just as he'd been in Colorado — relaxed and sweet.

We talked. For a few wonderful moments, it was as if I'd gone back in time.

Then reality hit.

Matt left and continued on his travels, not sure where he would go next, while I needed to stay right where I was.

I never saw him again.

Years later, I'd remember him when I visited supermarkets — every time I passed some bottles of Bolla wine.

Little doors

Your mindset can change in a split second. Lights come on and little doors swing open in your head. One day during my year in the rehabilitation center, a man whizzed by me in an electric wheelchair. He was dressed for work, with a gray suit and tie. I watched him disappear along the hall.

I went over to one of the nurses. "Who is he?" I asked.

"Oh, he's a psychologist who works on the fourth floor."

He is a psychologist? I thought. *Amazing.*

Money for nothing

Stacy and I were bored. Real bored.

We'd been roommates in the rehab center for several months. Stacy had Guillain-Barre Syndrome. She was a beautiful, fit, sixteen year-old from an affluent family who came down with a fever one night. A few hours later, she was paralyzed from her head to her toes. Her prognosis was good. She had a realistic chance of regaining 95% of her muscle function within twelve months. For the time being, though, we were both unable to walk and had a lot of time on our hands.

One hot day in Manhattan, we decided to have some fun. We were both finished with our physical therapy. We had no visitors, and we were sick of television.

"Hey Stacy, let's go outside and sell lemonade. Do you think anyone would buy any from us?"

Stacy was amused by the idea. Two girls in wheelchairs on 34th Street and 2nd Avenue, one of the busiest intersections in Manhattan, selling lemonade? What a crack up!

We went up to the occupational therapy department on the fifth floor and stole (well, borrowed) two pitchers, some lemonade mix and some ice. We filled the pitchers with cold water and took a stack of paper cups from the closet. Somehow, we managed to convince a volunteer to carry a small wooden table outside for us.

We were in business, and called out to the passing throng.

"Lemonade! Fifty cents!"

Hundreds of people passed by—stockbrokers, mothers with strollers, models, men in suits, women in fancy outfits and high heels. They glanced at us and walked on by, in the rushed fashion of all New Yorkers.

It was very hot, thirsty weather, but no one stopped to buy.

"Fresh- made lemonade, only fifty cents!" We called louder, but there were still no buyers.

Soon we lost interest and stopped shouting. We filled up a few of the cups and just sat there, not caring, talking about other things.

Suddenly, it was a whole new ball game. The minute we stopped selling was the minute we started taking money.

A man approached and dropped a couple of coins into an empty cup.

"Hey, you forgot to take some lemonade," I yelled after him. He wasn't interested.

They came in a steady stream, producing nickels, dimes and quarters—even dollars. No one took their lemonade. No one stopped to talk to us, or to laugh with us, but the money kept flowing.

Our cups runneth over.

No longer amused, we packed up our lemonade stand and headed back to the rehab center.

"Guess they thought we looked kind of pathetic," Stacy said with a wry smile.

"Yup," I replied. "At least it was better than another day of television."

Separate ways

"You left me, you went away."

Mark was right. I'd gone to Colorado.

He had been with someone else. I'd known it would happen, but I couldn't help crying.

"It didn't mean anything," Mark said quietly. It was a famous line, but I knew he genuinely felt remorse.

We'd tried to stay together, but it wasn't to be. We were very different people, and neither of us was ready to settle down. I was outgoing and adventurous, and I loved being surrounded by new people and things. Mark was more of a loner, wanting a simple, quiet life. Nova Scotia had been *his* dream, not mine.

After a year back in New York, I realized I still yearned for the new experiences I'd hoped to have by going to Colorado. I needed to see what and who was out there. I also now needed to prove to myself that I was still attractive, even in my wheelchair or walking awkwardly with two canes.

But Mark was my first love. He was there for me when it counted the most, and he had even changed his study major to orthotics and prosthetics. Years later, he made my first set of leg braces.

We went our separate ways, but remained friends. Mark has been married and divorced, and has two adult children. I have seen him every couple of years, when I return to New York.

Decades later, I'd be working on my computer when his name would appear in my instant messaging box. He talked to me as he did when I was sixteen. Sometimes, we still teased each other about who left who.

"Susan, why did you leave me? Why did you go to Colorado?"

"Why were you with that blonde waitress in upstate New York?" I'd reply.

We both knew that it didn't really matter anymore, but we both kept asking.

3.

I'd watch the students playing volleyball outside my dorm window. I'd watch the girls on my floor laugh and giggle as they left to go to Chinatown for some midnight spare ribs. I'd watch the friends I thought I had ignore me as they planned to go on the subway to catch a movie, knowing I couldn't use subways because of the hundreds of steps. I had become a spectator.

Love in New York City

I was obsessed with Andy. After a year of rehab, I had enrolled at New York University in the heart of Greenwich Village. Andy was a conceited young film student whose dorm room was just a few feet away from mine. He was tall, lean and blond. I loved hearing him talk about films and music, and I'd hang on his every word. He took me to small dark movie theaters to see experimental movies that I didn't really understand.

Andy said things like "special moments are frozen in time". To the ears of a newly disabled woman who needed to know she was still okay, banalities fell like jewels from his lips.

I felt like Pavlov's dog every time he knocked on the door of my room. Fresh out of the rehab center, my bladder barely working, I raced in my wheelchair to the bathroom. I quickly took off my pads, the disgusting white cloths I needed because my bladder acted like a two year-old's. *This is the night*, I would think as I prepared for the seduction, excited yet apprehensive about an experience I'd never had in my new, strange body.

Andy barged through the door as I emerged from the bathroom. I'm sure he had no idea about my routine of removing pads. At times, I wanted to tell him about my bladder, but the words had stuck in my throat.

Andy sat on my bed. *This is it*, I thought.

The long-anticipated dream was turning into reality. It was scary to think about my too-skinny legs, my too-nervous bladder and my too-freaky spasms, like little earthquakes. Surely, those would scare him off.

After a few awkward moments, I knew something was wrong. He was hesitant, unsure.

"Andy," I said finally, fearing rejection. "What's wrong? I know something is wrong."

"It's my first time," he said.

I smiled. It was a smile that enveloped my entire being. Inside, I was shaking with laughter.

Never again would I fear that someone suave and confident knew more than me, or that I wasn't worth as much as the tall, perfect girl in the high-heeled shoes I would never wear.

"Just leave it to me, Andy," I told him, as my spasmy body became the teacher of Mr. Cool.

Damaged goods

Being obsessed with Andy helped take my mind off the fact that I was now disabled, and no longer in Colorado climbing mountains.

Soon Andy decided to make a short documentary about me for one of his film classes. His camera rolled as I went around Greenwich Village, doing ordinary things in everyday life.

I attended the viewing of Andy's eight-minute film, the lecture hall filled with students, none of whom knew that I was sitting in the back row. After the film was over, the students and professors critiqued the film. Their comments were unanimous.

"That woman," they said, "is a terrible actress. She obviously isn't disabled, even though you try to make her look that way with her wheelchair and crutches."

"She's too happy. It is not believable. You should have used a real disabled person, or a better actress."

Still in the back row, I was thinking: *bizarre.*

What does a real disabled person look like? What did they think?

I probably looked so happy because I got to spend the day with Andy. At the time, I'd probably have given up a few years of my life if I thought it would make Andy keep liking me.

How stupid. Andy was like most of the men I would meet. Many would be interested and intrigued by me, and some would even venture to sleep with me. But they wouldn't want me for real. I was damaged goods. When their curiosity was satisfied, they'd go find their real girlfriends.

Watching

So much watching. Some people watched me, while I seemed to always be watching other people doing things that I'd have liked to do.

Being a spectator didn't suit me, but I just didn't have other people with disabilities to talk to. *Is this just the way it is,* I thought, *the way it has to be?*

No. I didn't buy that line of reasoning. I rejected it.

I wasn't depressed, and I no longer hated what had happened to me.

I didn't feel sorry for myself.

I didn't wish I was someone else.

These were the feelings other people seemed to *expect* me to have. Maybe those were *their* truths, the feelings that *they* would have if they wound up in a wheelchair at the age of eighteen. But not me. I didn't hate my atrophied legs or my malfunctioning bladder, and I didn't wish I was someone else.

I did, however, feel the discomfort of those around me. I started to get used to hearing this: "I like you but..."

Even worse, people seemed to love asking weird questions.

"What happened to you?"

"Can you feel anything?"

These people didn't even know me. They just stopped me in the street. What if I asked them whether they were divorced? What if I asked them whether they had sex last night? Who gave *them* the right to ask me all those personal questions? Was I just an object for their curiosity?

I pondered a theory that only misfits and perverts talk to

disabled people. One day I was walking slowly with my crutches through Greenwich Village when my awkward gait caught the attention of a man in his fifties. He followed me and began a conversation. I couldn't speed up to get rid of him.

"Where do you live," he began. "If I touch you, would you feel anything? You must be lonely."

I tried ignoring him, but he followed me anyway. After several very uncomfortable minutes, I was able to enter a university building and he disappeared.

Unfortunately, that kind of experience wasn't uncommon during my year at New York University. And perhaps there was some truth to the fact that I was, at times, lonely. On weekends, when my friends from before my accident were busy, I was alone.

I sat and watched.

I went to the park by the famous Washington Arch, watching all the folk singers and hippies of the day. Wanting so much to make new friends, I struck up conversation with a man in his thirties who said he'd served time for murder, but was now on parole. He was intelligent, and treated me with respect. When he explained that he needed to write a paper, I gave him the use of my new electric typewriter.

I never saw him or the typewriter again.

Looking back, I could see that a man who had murdered someone might not have been the wisest choice as a new friend.

Who am I now?

I became friends with Andy's sidekick. He was a curly-haired dentistry student who kidded me like a sister. He would come by my room before dinner, and we'd go down the hall to ride the elevator to the basement cafeteria. We'd laugh when we noticed people staring at me. We'd eat dinner, chatting about lousy food and unfair professors. Having a friend in the dorms brought some semblance of normalcy.

One Saturday night, in a room just down the hall, someone made orange juice cocktails laced with vodka. It was a typical student binge, and I wanted to be part of it. After throwing up in my room for several hours, I vowed never to get so drunk again— and it was a promise I kept.

My throwing up was nothing compared to the students taking uppers and downers. You'd see them sleeping in the halls or bouncing off the walls babbling esoteric nonsense.

It was a world I didn't feel part of.

I went to class, took notes, studied and crammed. That was all okay, but it wasn't an easy time. There was a voice in my head saying, *it's only for a year.* I was still hoping to continue my quest to live out west, away from New York. I was planning another life.

Studying in New York had never been my intention so I felt disoriented, and not having a solid sense of identity compounded the problem. I was never the artist, the cook, the knitter, the pianist, the singer, and I was no longer the fast runner, the strong climber, the fluid dancer. Everything I was good at was gone.

Who was I now?

I didn't know. I didn't have the answer, and there was nobody who could help me find it. Least of all, Andy. He dumped me to have a real girlfriend, and I went on vacation with my parents.

Club Med

We went to Club Med in the beautiful Caribbean. It was perfection. Perfect bodies, perfect muscles. Perfect features, perfect tans. Everybody played sports in perfect sunshine, and had perfect sex at night.

Maybe, though, it wasn't the perfect place to stretch out on the beach with my atrophied legs covered by knee-high socks and braces. I was the only crip at the resort, and doubted whether knee-high socks would ever be in vogue with bathing suits. I watched people watch me, and knew what they were thinking.

I moved only a few steps from my wheelchair. I walked slowly on the beach with my two canes, swaying back and forth like a drunk gorilla. I was slower than an arthritic woman of ninety. What made it hard for people to avoid staring was that I looked so young.

I *was* so young, barely twenty years old.

They felt bad for me.

Little did they know that I wasn't as miserable as they thought. I was smiling inside, thinking about a man I met on the plane. He was a cowboy from Colorado, short and strong with blond hair and stream-blue eyes. We sparkled with each other, and had arranged to meet one night.

My Club Med roommate, a thirty year-old woman from Manhattan, gave me some advice. "Hang the bathing suit on the doorknob outside," she said. "It's the signal you use to let people know that you need privacy."

Meaning, of course, sex. Club Med is *the* place for wild flings, and I needed to know local customs. Like the big sister I never had, my roommate also talked to me about the benefits of Clairol hair conditioner.

Excitement about the night kept building. I was preparing myself for a ride with the Colorado cowboy. The trouble was, I couldn't get the diaphragm in. I couldn't lift my leg up high enough, or spread my legs easily. My legs just didn't do that. I tried squatting on the toilet and slipping the diaphragm in while sitting.

It was full of jelly. *I* was full of jelly. It was crazy. The diaphragm slipped out of my fingers. Like a flying saucer, it zapped across the bathroom.

I tried again.

And again, and again.

Finally, the mission was accomplished. I checked, just to be sure. It was hard to tell whether I'd found the pubic bone that it was supposed to be resting on.

I checked again.

My heart rate increased tenfold as I went out the door.

He was all dressed up and looked even nicer than I remembered. We went to the beach and talked about horses, ranches and life. It was romantic. It was Club Med. Perfection. The perfect fling — the fling I was supposed to have.

We kissed. His tongue flickered in my mouth, exciting and mysterious. My heart beat faster. We went back to my room, moving toward the inevitable. My bathing suit was hanging on the doorknob. The scene was set.

Yes, he was sweet. But for a woman starting to reclaim her sexuality, there was a much more intoxicating thought: he wanted me.

Somebody wants me.

This handsome man was attracted to me — atrophied legs, braces and all. There were gorgeous young women everywhere, with high heels and red-painted toenails. But he had picked me.

"I can't do this to you," he said. He caught his breath. It was like he was making an effort to stop, going against inner drives.

"Why not?"

I was deflated. I was also annoyed, remembering the hours it took to get my stupid diaphragm in.

"Because you're disabled, and I will hurt your feelings."

"But I want you to be with me tonight. I know it's just for tonight and we may never see each other again."

"I'm sorry, I just can't. It wouldn't be fair to you. I'm afraid I'll hurt you, and it wouldn't be right. We can be friends. I'm sorry, I just can't. Not with you."

He gave me a peck on the forehead and walked away.

He left me in tears. I wanted him.

Well, maybe it wasn't so much *him* that I wanted — after all, we'd only been together three hours. I liked him, but what I really wanted was my wild fling. I wanted to feel as attractive as I once was. I wanted to feel the same as those high-heeled women that all the guys turned their heads to see.

But I wasn't. This was an era when disabled women were seen as non-sexual beings. This was an era when disabled women were people to take care of and feel sorry for. It wasn't ready for me.

A few years later, I returned to Club Med on another family vacation. It was no longer unusual to see a woman in a wheelchair. There had been movies depicting paraplegics as sexual beings — regrettably, only men — and disabled rights were at last being discussed in the news. People stared, but not so unashamedly. People didn't ask as many stupid questions. Things were changing for the better.

After my parents went to sleep, I stayed up and had a few drinks in the bar. It didn't take me long to feel a bit tipsy. A tall man with deep dark eyes asked me to dance. He then suggested we go skinny dipping in the warm ocean. I felt his strong arms around me and my bathing suit top slip off.

"Let's go to my room," he suggested.

I remembered my rejection several years earlier.

"Why not?"

Once in his room, I felt a little embarrassed. "I'm shy," I told him. "This is not something I do often."

He looked at me with wry disbelief. "You are completely undressed, and we are about to have sex after knowing each other for about one hour, and you want me to believe you are shy?"

Let's just say he completed the task. I didn't feel much in the way of fulfillment or excitement, but I had a smile on my face. I'd just been used — like any other woman. Things had changed.

I felt great. And I remember thinking: *Sleeping with someone after knowing them for a few hours? Never, ever again!*

Moving on

New York University had never been my destination. It was a stopping point on my way to the college life I'd always dreamed about.

But where could I go? Not Colorado. I didn't want to return

there as a student. Colorado was a place for rock climbing and skiing, an episode of my life that had ended far too quickly. I'd had my transition year living in Greenwich Village and it was time to move on. I wanted to continue my journey.

I wanted somewhere exotic and exciting, far from home. I hoped to continue my studies in recreation and recreational therapy, but now I was more like the people I had wanted to help. There were also practical issues to consider, like wheelchair accessibility. It wasn't just about pretty universities and sports offerings any more. Yes, I wanted to go to a good school with challenging classes and innovative thinkers. But could I get around the campus? Could I get into the classrooms? What about the bathrooms?

Was any of this possible?

My self concept had been bruised. No, *maimed*.

During my year in New York, I had applied for part-time jobs. I wanted to work in a department store, but people looked at me as though I was from the moon. People in wheelchairs are not salespeople. Didn't I know that?

I hit rock bottom when I answered an advertisement for a telemarketing job. When I entered the room for my interview, the woman looked at me and said, "Oh you must be applying for the handicapped job."

"No," I replied. "I came here to apply for the telemarketing job advertised in the newspaper."

"Yes, of course, I understand," she stated flatly. "But you will need to go to the room where the handicapped people work."

Although I was infuriated, I didn't know what to do or say. There didn't seem to be much choice. I'd been refused for so many jobs. I was desperate. I followed the woman into a room filled with people in wheelchairs, each in their own little cubicle, talking on the phone.

"What are they doing?" I asked.

"Selling pencils. Here is the script."

I looked at the piece of paper I had been handed. In a nutshell, the script said, "Hello, I'm handicapped and I'm raising money so I'd really like you to buy some pencils."

"I need to think about this," I said.

Part of me was saying *take this job*—you won't get any other. The other part of me was outraged. There was a voice in my head and it was shouting at me: *I can't believe you are even thinking about selling pencils on the phone by telling people that you are "handicapped"!*

When I woke up the next morning, I realized how damaged my sense of self had become. I read somewhere that Eleanor Roosevelt said that people can only make you feel inferior if you give them consent to do it. I'm not sure what I think about this statement. In order not to give consent, you need to know that you are worth something.

Deep inside, I knew I was worth something, but I was surrounded by messages telling me I was inferior.

Unattractive.

Unemployable.

I constantly felt left out of life because I could not get on the bus or the subway or play sports.

My parents wanted me to feel proud of who I was, and to be optimistic. But for all their positive thinking, there was a part of me that even they couldn't embrace. It was hard for them to see me in my wheelchair. I could walk only a few steps with my canes, but like other people they preferred to see me use them than my wheelchair.

One day, I was on a shopping trip with my mother. I was in my wheelchair, holding my two canes on my lap. We were in a bookstore and my mom saw one of her friends.

"Get out of your wheelchair," she said, wanting to show her friend that I really could walk a little.

"Why?" I responded. "Why can't I stay in my wheelchair? I'm not getting up."

My feelings were hurt. I was mad. *Mommy*, I thought, *why can't you accept that I am in a wheelchair? I feel free in my wheelchair. I can move around quickly. I can carry things. This is me.*

But I never said what I was thinking. For my parents, a wheelchair was a negative. It was a sign of immobility, not mobility. My mom and dad had no mental images or models of thinking that accommodated wheelchairs in a positive light. It wasn't their fault. They were doing their best.

Often I would hear my mom say, "Put the deckchair in the car." I knew she meant wheelchair. But a deckchair conjured pleasant thoughts of the beach, or a cruise ship, so I never corrected her slip.

Inside, I knew that this way of thinking was all wrong. *I* was not the problem. No, I *wasn't*. I was essentially the same person that had climbed into Faisal's car — except that I was now in a wheelchair. Somewhere, I imagined, there must be others that know this. There must be others who think this way, and others still who have dreams that everyone could think this way.

And then I heard of a place called Berkeley.

The University of California at Berkeley.

Sunny California. Home of hippies and free speech. Home to a university with a program for disabled students, a university that didn't make me apply to a 'rehabilitation unit' for admission. It didn't have my major, or any courses in recreation, but that didn't matter.

I sensed that it had what I needed. It was far away, exotic. *Yes*, I thought. Berkeley sounded like the perfect place for a fresh start.

And that's exactly what it turned out to be.

4.

There was the buzz of new ideas. Nothing was too crazy for Berkeley. Every Sunday, I went to little cafes and ate banana crepes. I was meeting fascinating people, spending hours talking about politics, astrophysics, literature and revolution. There was even someone in the free speech plaza selling land on the moon for a dollar an acre.

Berkeley

Curb cuts were everywhere. Well, maybe not everywhere—but in more places than I had ever seen before. I flew around the streets in my wheelchair, pushing fast with attitude.

No stopping me!

Up and down Telegraph Avenue, past the street vendors selling bright colored scarves, hash pipes, beaded bracelets and leather moccasins. No one stared at me.

This was *not* New York.

People with disabilities had come to Berkeley from all over the United States. I saw a man with light brown hair crossing the street in a power wheelchair. He maneuvered his chair with a head stick fastened around his forehead. By the way his arms were tightly folded around his body, his fists clenched tight, it seemed like he had cerebral palsy. He was smiling, with a slight drool coming from his mouth. He sped across the road, passing the slower, able-bodied people who had to get out of his way. Before he disappeared from view, I saw a sign fastened to the back of his wheelchair. It was written in big block letters: "I'm proud to be a crip."

That says it all, I thought.

Disability wonderland

I moved to Berkeley, sight unseen. The university had accepted me, saying that once I'd arrived I could apply for resident status and get funding — not only for tuition but also for a golf cart to get around in.

Golf cart? I'd never heard of such a thing — away from a golf course, at least. Yes, the people at the disabled student services office had said, I could use my wheelchair. But the campus was hilly, and a golf cart would be helpful. I could throw my wheelchair into the back of it and happily cruise anywhere.

Incredible, I thought. *I don't have to figure everything out for myself.*

It was such a new concept. I'd never really imagined that these kinds of support systems existed, and initially experienced difficulty adjusting to the idea that others could solve problems for me.

The disabled students' program was actually *run* by disabled people. Quadriplegics were everywhere — running programs, getting their PhDs, holding parties and sleeping with beautiful people, disabled or not.

I felt like Dorothy in the *Wizard of Oz*. It sure wasn't Kansas. I'd arrived in a disability wonderland.

Climate of change

I lived in a dormitory housing mostly law students. I was on the ground floor with an accessible bathroom. For some unknown reason, they had put some of the freshmen football team on the same floor. Mammoth young men walked around in their underwear, playing silly tricks on each other. The air was thick with body odor, booming laughter and pounding music. My first roommate, who later became a disability advocate, soon moved out. She was a law student and couldn't study with all the ruckus.

I liked it. It was never boring, and the guys were very helpful. Little did I know that some of them would one day become rich and famous national football stars!

I was happy in Berkeley. I took an independent major because there wasn't a recreation department, and I designed my own curriculum with the help of an adviser. My major was called "Conservation of Natural Resources". People were talking about environmental concerns — recycling and oil monopolies. They were twenty years ahead of the rest of the world.

For a course in environmental education, I decided to design a wheelchair accessible garden for disabled kids attending a nearby school. I wanted the kids to build the garden themselves. I wanted them to get shovels and hammers and paintbrushes in their hands. I wanted them to make it their own.

No one ever asks disabled kids to do things like other kids. People are always cushioning them, giving them charity.

I applied for some funding from the city council to cover the cost of materials. I convinced a bluegrass band to volunteer their time to provide entertainment while the kids and teachers spent the day building their own garden. It was designed so that they could get their hands muddy and filthy and smell the plants without having to get out of their wheelchairs.

What a fabulous day!

What I didn't realize at the time was that I had just begun a career of creating projects to empower disabled people. In fact, "empower" wasn't even in my vocabulary. It was all about having fun.

At Berkeley, the professors I had didn't care much about grades. We met in small cafés at the end of the term, and I came with pages of notes about all the things I had done in my independent major.

"Susan," they said, "stop right there. You don't have to convince me you did all those things. I know you have. I'm here to ask you what you have *learned*."

I was amazed.

This was how I'd always dreamed university life could be. Of course, not all my professors took that approach, but many did. They were innovative. They trusted that I would take responsibility for learning whatever I needed to learn. There was no separation between school and life.

People in Berkeley were there to change the world.

And there was a world of people to change.

Olive Oyl

I found myself searching for role models. I had a new body and had started to embrace a new life, but role models were few and far between.

The closest thing I could think of was Olive Oyl, the cartoon girlfriend of Popeye the Sailor Man. She had tight black hair pulled back in a ponytail. She wore a red shirt over black skirt and, protruding from the black skirt, had legs like mine! They were long and tubular in shape, like two lengths of pipe. There were no obvious thighs or calves. Olive Oyl's legs seemed atrophied, but she never seemed ashamed of them.

Okay, so she had a flat chest. In that, we were different—but, for now, I decided, she could be my role model.

I also liked the giant peanut man on the label of Planter's nuts. He was dressed in a tuxedo and used a cane, but seemed jolly and relaxed. No disability complex for him! No hiding his cane!

Olive Oyl and the peanut man. They were the start of a list of new heroes and heroines.

I was looking to add to it.

Mind over bladder

I can't believe she did that.

That is what I thought when I heard Debbie speak about her "little episode" during a law school class. She was an attractive, smart and slightly smug woman with sharp eyes, short brown hair and a strong personality. She'd broken her neck and was an unusual quadriplegic, able to walk with a cane but with paralysis on half of her body.

We were sitting in a circle somewhere in Berkeley, a group of women with disabilities who had gathered to tell our stories — the problems, the passions, the prejudices. It was an encounter group — we called it a "rap" group. It was fun, and a sense of camaraderie had developed. We were sowing the seeds for a thought revolution by women with disabilities around the world.

Debbie was doing first year law, studying torts. Like most of us, she had a weak bladder resulting from a spinal cord injury. It was unpredictable, with a mind of its own. Nobody in the group had talked about bladders before. It was something we hid — shamefully.

Not Debbie!

She told us that, toward the end of one recent class, she realized that her bladder had emptied. A large yellow puddle had formed around her chair. All of us listening to her story registered our horror.

"So what did you do?"

We tried to imagine ourselves in that situation. What would *we* do?

There was a smirk on Debbie's face. "I raised my hand. I said, 'I have just peed on the floor and, being that I can't clean it up myself, I suggest that a few people get some paper towels and clean it up for me. Thank you.'"

Silence.

I stared at Debbie in amazement.

"You really said that?" I asked.

Unbelievable.

Slowly, the attitude behind Debbie's story sank in, and when it did we were a different group. At first it had seemed no more than a simple, embarrassing incident—but it was so much more than that. A paradigm shift. *We* were not the problem. Our bladders were not *responsible*.

We should not be embarrassed.

We should not be ashamed.

We should not need to apologize.

We were fine—exactly the way we were. Suddenly, we felt that it was okay to be proud women with disabilities. Our atrophied legs, our leaky bladders and our gnarled fingers were okay. Our spasmy bodies were okay.

They were *ours*.

My mind went back to all the times I had been embarrassed by my bladder… Hiding the reality of it from Andy, the ultra cool filmmaker down the hall at New York University… Buying diapers in the supermarket but telling the guy at the checkout counter that it was for a little sister… Asking for a glass of water in a restaurant, and deliberately spilling it on my lap to disguise a dirty secret...

The list went on.

Now I realized that there was another way. I needed to learn to live my life in this new body without shame or frustration. It would take boldness and a sense of humor, but it was possible.

Years later, when I set out to travel the world, I would have to find ways to "go to the bathroom" at a moment's notice, often in places where there was no wheelchair access, and often in places where there was no toilet at all.

I learned how to maneuver my body to pee off the front of my chair, supporting myself with my arms.

I peed near the Eiffel Tower on a beautiful, starry night when there was no bathroom in sight. I was discreet, holding a sweater over my knees so passers-by wouldn't notice – but I was not ashamed.

I peed on a snowcapped mountain trail on the glaciers of New Zealand.

I peed on the Great Wall of China while leading a group of twenty-five disabled people on a tour.

I always carried an extra pair of pants with me (the same color as the ones I was wearing) so that I was ready for all possibilities.

But I did not hide. I would not be embarrassed. And I would share my convictions with other disabled women around the world. It all started with that one story from Debbie. It isn't possible to talk about a revolution of ideas — about human rights and equality — when there is shame about who you are.

Loud, Proud and Passionate. Much later, that would be the motto of a program bringing disabled women together from all over the world. I had stared at Debbie with wonder. Later, other women would stare at me.

"You really did that?"

"Yes," I would tell them. "And I'm proud of it."

Rod

At the rehab center in New York, no one ever talked to me about body image, or sex, or anything like that. The only messages I received — in one short, hushed conversation — were that I could still have children if I wanted, and could "please a man" if I found someone who wanted me.

Please a man.

That's nice, I thought. What about me?

I guess I didn't count any more. Being only eighteen at the time of my accident, my explorations of sex had been fairly limited. There was now an expectation that it would remain that way — and neither Andy nor Club Med had provided compelling reasons to hope otherwise.

In Berkeley, however, I was surrounded by a new way of thinking and being. Anything seemed possible. I was meeting people who didn't know me before I was disabled.

One of those people was Rod.

Rod had turquoise eyes and thick blond hair that flowed around his face to his shoulders. He was from rural Nevada — a place called Elko. He was shy, and spoke slowly and carefully, always in the background of conversations, never drawing attention to himself. He was a Vietnam veteran, and had completed his tour of duty unharmed, happy to be relieved from service to a cause he didn't believe in.

Weeks after his return to Nevada, he was involved in a motorcycle accident that left him a high paraplegic — paralyzed from just beneath his nipples right down to his toes. Rod's wife left him after his accident, and he was devastated and depressed. Relationship breakdown after a traumatic accident is very common — it's more common for men to leave disabled women, but able bodied women also leave newly disabled men.

When I met Rod, he worked in an independent living center in Berkeley, fixing wheelchairs and teaching other disabled folks how to fix their own. He was always tinkering with his own chair, getting just the right axle and camber — things I had barely begun to learn about. Rod was a strong man. After his accident, his legs and arms did not seem to have atrophied, unlike those of most people who have been disabled for a while. If standing, he would probably have been about six feet tall.

Independent living centers were a revolutionary concept. They were non-profit organizations run by and for disabled people based on a human rights model — not a medical model. These centers had lots of people in wheelchairs buzzing around telling people how to get their benefits (what to say and what *not* to say), how to get the government to pay for college or university, how to find an accessible apartment, or how to find a personal assistant if you needed help with dressing or bathing. They addressed all the issues that needed to be addressed if disabled people were to live independently.

I don't know why I caught Rod's eye, but I think I do know why he caught mine. It was partly that I liked his quiet bearing, his startling eyes and his blond hair. And it was partly that I was searching for someone who would accept and love the new me.

Rod took me for a drink in a high rise hotel in San Francisco. I was at the mercy of his eyes, his Nevada accent, and the way he called me "Sooz". There was a beautiful view, and he held my hand. It was his touch that made me fall in love with him.

Sometimes while we were talking to friends, I would use my canes and stand up next to my wheelchair, and he would reach out and hold me around my wobbly knees. He caressed me, slowly. What Rod didn't communicate in words, he did through his touch.

Rod was my first lover with a disability and oh, how that

changed things. He had no control of his heavy legs, and had to maneuver them into bed. He used an out-dwelling catheter to catch his urine, carefully wrapping it around his penis as part of his morning routine. He cursed and swore when there was a leak or something else was wrong.

I learned about adapting to my disability through watching Rod adapt to his. He taught me how to jump curbs in my wheelchair, gathering up speed and then doing a wheelie on the big back tires so that the chair leaped over huge obstacles.

Rod was the master. He could go up and down escalators in his chair, a skill I could never quite learn. He could go down a flight of stairs in his chair by balancing on his back wheels and dropping them down, step by step. And he never allowed anyone to push him up a hill — no matter how steep. He would simply crisscross the incline until he got to the top, no matter how long it took or how arduous. Rod was as stubborn as he was strong. He was proud.

And he was a great lover.

We spent hours making love. Somehow he knew where to touch me and how to touch me — even though I was still uncertain about the level of sensation I had on different parts of my body. He seemed to pick up the slightest nuances. Was it my breathing? I don't know.

Rod was a revelation.

He knew what I wanted, and what my body needed.

5.

There was a big decision to make. I was in a San Francisco building with over a hundred protesters, mostly disabled. It was a sit-in. We didn't know it at the time, but it was the longest takeover of any US federal building. This was history in the making, yet I was preoccupied with a decision that was personal.

Doing it for real

"Why not submit this to the city council and start this program, Susan?"

My professor's direct question momentarily stunned me. I was just a student doing a class assignment.

"Huh?" It wasn't the most brilliant response, but my professor didn't seem to be discouraged.

"You've thought of everything. Why not just do it for real?"

I hadn't thought of that. I was flattered, but unsure. I decided to think about it.

We'd been talking about some ideas I'd outlined for a recreation program for people with disabilities.

Not therapy — *recreation*.

When I came to Berkeley and asked about doing some

swimming, I was directed to a "therapeutic" swimming program. Why were disabled people always considered to be sick, to be in need of a cure, to want therapy? Why couldn't I just go to a local pool, get in the water, and enjoy swimming like everyone else?

Yes, disabled people need accessible bathrooms and changing facilities, ramps if possible, and a hydraulic lift to help with getting into the water. Yes, there should also be a person available to assist if required. What I didn't understand is why all that wasn't possible.

I had already designed a wheelchair accessible garden for disabled kids at a local school, and now I'd been asked to design a program or service needed in the community. I thought of my irritation about being told to go to a therapeutic swimming class, when all I really wanted was to sink my body into some cool water and use my strong arms to swim laps. I thought of all my other frustrations in trying to access opportunities in recreation.

The thoughts got bigger, and bolder. I started to conceive of a non-therapeutic recreation program run by and for disabled people. I dreamed of a program in which disabled people were not thought of as sick or needy, and were simply provided with opportunities to swim, dance, go camping and play sports.

For me, it all seemed so obvious. In essence, I was imagining a recreation program like the one I would have wanted to go to when I was seventeen — before I was in a wheelchair. Was that so complicated?

I could find a local pool and look at ways of making the bathroom more accessible. Someone could be hired to help people getting into the pool, or out of it, and also with dressing if that was required. A swim teacher could get involved — not necessarily one

56

who knew anything about disabled folks because I could help adapt the lessons, and we could also get input from those who came along to the sessions. After all, why not ask disabled people themselves — they are the experts when it comes to their own needs. I was getting excited. This could work!

What else would I want to do?

I'd always loved dancing. Why not have modern dance classes in my apartment? We could get everyone down on the floor, or in their chairs, and get a modern dance teacher who knows nothing about disability but loves dance with a passion. We could play some great music and get those atrophied legs and amputated stumps moving. We could rock out — or we could explore slow, graceful movements.

We could have fun, and regain love for our bodies.

We could stretch.

Inhale.

This could happen.

My mind raced. The possibilities were endless. Camping in the Yosemite Mountains. Getting a van with a lift so that folks in chairs could easily get in. Finding a place to camp where there was a power supply, so that those who used electric wheelchairs could plug in for the night and recharge. Researching the most accessible trails. Having sleeping bags donated, and cots available under shelter for those needing a little more comfort.

Freedom in the outdoors. I could smell the burgers, see the ketchup, taste marshmallows melting over chocolate and graham crackers after being toasted under the stars.

I thought about sports. A wheelchair basketball team. Gymnastics. That's what *I'd* like to do — surely others would, too! I could get permission from the University of California's Berkeley gymnasium and enlist some teachers. We'd do stretches. Use weights, parallel bars, and ropes. We'd get into shape — the same way the athletes do, in the same gym, side-by-side with those non-disabled folks.

Why not?

There could also be a program for kids with spinal cord injury or cerebral palsy. There could be disabled coaches. Role models. Mentors.

It might have started as a project for class — but it was becoming so much more than that.

The professor was right. I could do it for real.

Pobrecita?

My parents were not thrilled that my new boyfriend was a paraplegic. Why would I want a man who was paralyzed?

When I told them that Rod and I were planning a trip to Mexico by ourselves, they were horrified. Who would carry my bags? Who would help me? Didn't I know that Mexico wouldn't be wheelchair accessible? How could I do this with *him*?

However, my mom and dad must also have sensed that I was happy, that I had found a new sense of self. Having voiced their disagreement and displeasure, they acknowledged that I needed to live my own life. They could not stop me from making my own decisions, and they needed to trust my judgment.

So off to Mexico we went.

Rod and I each had a large backpack carefully strapped to

the back of our wheelchairs, fastened by carabineers used for rock climbing. We carried a small day pack under our wheelchairs, held in place by mesh canvas, which helped to balance our weight. Short of money, we took a thirty-five hour train from San Francisco to Guadalajara.

A friend had been able to get us the use of a beautiful villa in Puerto Vallarta, and we had a view of the sea. There were housekeepers who cooked fresh red snapper in the evenings. We made love while hearing light rain gently patter on rooftops.

I learned that I could travel again, and traveling with Rod made me know that I didn't need any able bodied people to help me. I stopped feeling that I needed to apologize because I was slower getting around, or needed more time in the bathroom, or took longer getting dressed.

Rod and I were a team, and had an understanding based on shared experience. We solved problems together.

When no local bus would stop for us, we went to the city bus station and talked to the bus drivers at the point of origin. They were always surprised and hesitant, but we were insistent. Rod climbed up the stairs of the bus on his rear end, and I crawled up slowly grabbing at the hand rails. Everyone stared at these unusual Americans. They protested, but we wouldn't back down. They threw our wheelchairs up to the roof of the buses with their live chickens and fresh produce. We got to remote villages just as we had intended. Every once in a while, I caught a look of respect or admiration in an old man's eye, winking as if to say, "Live your life—be happy".

We were.

We were tanned, healthy and fit.

Yet, to most outsiders, we continued to be oddities. Two young people in wheelchairs? At least we had each other — the assumption, of course, being that no one else would want us.

One old Mexican woman, whose calloused fingers and hardened face testified to a difficult life, stopped me in the street one morning on the way to the market place.

"Pobrecita," she said. I translated silently: *Poor little thing*.

She gestured toward my paralyzed legs in the wheelchair.

"Las muertas." *Those dead ones*.

"Pobrecita," she repeated. There were tears in her eyes, and she patted me on the head like a sick little girl — or a lost puppy.

"I'm really fine," I said in fairly good Spanish. "Estoy muy bien. No problemas para mi — no se preocupe."

Clearly, she didn't believe me. She shook her head and slowly walked away.

Later that day, I went sailing with Rod. In the evening, we dined by candlelight overlooking the sea. We made love all night.

Pobrecita?

I don't think so!

The right to take risks

I loved the thought of creating something I believed in. The idea of a recreation program quickly took shape and I called Diane, a friend who was graduating in recreation in Colorado. Diane and I had lived a few blocks away from each other in New York, and had gone to high school together.

"What do you think, Diane?" I asked her. "Maybe we could

do it together? Start a recreation program?"

"Sure. Why not?" Diane immediately started making plans to come out to Berkeley.

In the meantime, I spoke to a confident acquaintance in his late twenties. He had several years of experience working in the therapeutic recreation field, and I thought he might be able to give some advice.

"Well, Susan," he said. "It sounds okay. I would be willing to help you out with my expertise. I could be the director, and run things." He paused for a moment, deep in thought. He looked worried, and I sensed that he'd thought of a very significant obstacle.

"What are you thinking?" I asked.

"Well, the problem is... How can I put this? We would need to hire a swim teacher, a dance teacher, a gymnastics teacher, and someone who could drive a van and lead and organize the trips. That wouldn't be too hard. That's manageable."

"I agree," I said, still no clearer about where the problem lay.

"But," he continued slowly, "I'm just not sure what exactly you could do. You couldn't physically help anyone in swimming, dance, gymnastics or the trips, and you have no experience. I'm not sure where we would put you, and how we could go about budgeting for a position you could fill."

I went into quiet shock. It was like being back in that telemarketing room, being told that all I could do was sell pencils by calling people and saying I was handicapped.

You want to know what I could do? I thought. *You want to know where you would put me? You must be joking. I'm the one who came up with the idea. I can organize the whole thing! I can write the proposal, lobby the city council, get the rooms, hire and train the teachers, run the publicity, recruit the disabled people. What could I do? You are a non-disabled guy telling me – a disabled woman – that you don't know what I could do? It's my idea and you are ready to jump in as director and have me what? Volunteer to stuff your envelopes?*

I'd like to claim that I responded with a great comeback, a memorable speech on discrimination and rights. I didn't. I said I would think about it, and left his office. I was in shock, and depressed.

That night I called Diane and told her what happened.

"We're going to do it, Susan," she said. "We'll be co-directors."

That sounded great. I started coming out of shock. You bet we would!

My anger began to surface. The gall of the man! What assumptions! What conceit! What total disregard for me – and probably all other disabled women who threatened his imagined superiority. I'd never again let anyone tell me I couldn't do something when I knew that I could. To hell with him!

Diane came to Berkeley. We wrote a proposal and presented it direct to the city council. In 1975, the Berkeley Outreach Recreation Program (BORP) received $17,000 to run recreation programs by and for disabled people. It was an exciting and challenging time.

One incident stands out in my mind because it revealed some of the attitudes that we were up against. We needed to change the way many people thought.

As co-director of BORP, I was in front of hundreds of people at a conference for recreation therapists from throughout the country. Like me, these people had chosen a profession in which they could help disabled people—but unlike most of them, I was also one of the people they had set out to help.

I was showing the audience a new saddle we had designed. It was the result of months of work by a team of disabled people, Stanford University rehab engineers, and "equestrian experts"—the guys who ran the local stables.

"So, as you can see, the saddle has a high back for people who have limited balance," I told them proudly. "We've got sheepskin padding on the seat to prevent pressure sores for people who have sensitive skin or poor blood circulation—so common with folks with spinal cord injuries—and don't know if the saddle is chafing them. There is also a harness with straps that run from the back of the saddle over the shoulders, with a quick release mechanism in front. This is for people with very limited balance, such as quadriplegics, who want to ride but need additional support because of weaker trunk muscles. We have built ramps at the local stables so that any disabled person can go riding whenever they are open. A few horses have been specially trained to respond to neck rein, for folks who can't use their legs to signal the horse. One horse is trained to stop if the reins are dropped—for additional safety."

A large man in his forties, dressed in a suit and tie, had raised his hand and was agitatedly trying to attract my attention. I had the feeling that he was not impressed by my presentation.

He finally got his chance. "How dare you put all these people at risk? This program is not a responsible therapeutic recreation program. What if the horse takes off in a gallop? What if the horse rolls, and the disabled person is pinned under the horse?

Someone could get killed. I'm surprised they let you present at this conference."

I let the man finish. The room fell still. People were uneasy. Without doubt, he had tapped into a sentiment shared by many others in the auditorium. They waited to hear my response. They were skeptical.

"Thank you for your question," I replied confidently. "Let me assure you that this program is designed for folks over twenty-one. It is for people who are looking to regain the joy and excitement they had before being disabled. Others may want to experience something new, something that they have been *over*protected from all their lives. We want to give disabled people a chance to be out in the woods, smelling the scent of pines in fresh air, going along trails that they could not otherwise access."

"But do they know how dangerous this could be for them?" This time, the question came from an older woman dressed in a red suit. Her face was painted over with concern.

"I asked that question to a friend of mine," I responded. "He is a young man who is a quadriplegic, and he helped us with the design of this saddle. He answered without a blink. 'Susan,' he said, 'every quadriplegic has the right to break his neck—*twice*.'"

There was a moment of absolute silence. It was eerie. There were hundreds of people not knowing exactly what others were thinking, not knowing how to react. No one moved, no one breathed. It was as if I'd thrown out a grenade and we were all uncertain whether it was going to explode.

Five seconds later, half the audience broke out in nervous laughter. Some remained stony faced. A few began to applaud.

The moderator, not sure whose side she was on, thanked the

audience and closed the session.

The point I was making was important. Shouldn't disabled people have the right to take the same risks as non-disabled people? Don't many non-disabled people choose to do dangerous things?

I co-directed the program with Diane for two years, and Diane continued to direct the program after me. BORP grew into a nationally recognized model and, three decades later, Diane and I received civic awards for being its founders.

Have faith in your ideas, follow your dreams.

Sometimes, they come true.

Section 504

To leave, or to stay?

It was 1977, and protesters had taken over the federal Department of Health, Education and Welfare building in San Francisco. I was committed to the cause, and was right in there with them. We had a sense of history and wanted to seize our moment. We were a force for change, demanding a better world for people with disabilities.

There were paraplegics, quads and amputees. There were people who were blind, and people who were Deaf. There were folks with developmental disabilities and parents of disabled kids. There were hundreds more of us outside.

But I had a problem. I had received word that I was a finalist in a very competitive selection process for a full Rotary Scholarship to study in Australia. If I missed the interview, held about two hours outside San Francisco, I would lose my chance.

What to do?

Our demonstration was aimed at forcing the President of the United States to sign the regulations of Section 504 of Rehabilitation Act 1973. It was the first disability civil rights law anywhere and, without the regulations being signed, it could not go into effect. The law would make it illegal for any federal agency, federal contractor or other entity receiving public funds to discriminate against anyone solely by reason of "handicap". That might sound like a lot of jargon, but it was jargon that would change the lives of millions of people in the United States. Later, it would be a model for other legislation throughout the world. When the Section 504 regulations were signed, universities, community colleges, schools, post offices, and all other institutions receiving as little as one cent of public money would need to make provision for people with disabilities.

The day all of us entered the building, no one took much notice. Surely, the thinking seemed to run, these disabled people would get tired and leave by the end of the day. But when the end of the day came, we locked our wheelchairs, grasped each other's hands and chanted.

"Hell no, we won't go! Hell no, we won't go!"

The officials were going to call the police, bring in the paddy wagons. But there was no way the police would come. Their cars didn't have wheelchair lifts, and the police officers were frightened of injuring these "fragile" disabled people and risking the possibility of being sued. Besides, if they arrested everyone, and had them go to jail, there were other problems to consider. Bathrooms at the police stations were not wheelchair accessible, and no one was trained to lift or drag a disabled person against their will.

There had always been an assumption that disabled people were passive, weak, quiet. Nothing like this had ever occurred before.

Ed Roberts, one of the many disability activists who planned the takeover – along with Pat Wright, Mary Lou Breslin, Judy Heumann and others – quoted Winston Churchill: "Never in the field of human conflict was so much owed by so many to so few." Ed reminded us: "Whenever we bring ourselves together, whenever we join various disabilities together, we find our strength. We know what we need to do — to help raise the consciousness of our fellow Americans with disabilities, to help them come out from behind, from the back wards, from the institutions, from the garbage heaps in our society. We have to stop the warehousing, the segregation of our brothers and sisters. We are no longer asking for charity. We are demanding our rights."

Those of us in the building had organized ourselves into committees. Some distributed food that had been donated by groups as diverse as McDonalds and the Black Panthers, a group of radical black activists. Some organized attendant care services for those in need of help with dressings, eating, or any other basic function. Some were dealing with the media, writing press releases and monitoring news coverage.

We were washing ourselves in basins and sinks. We were singing and making plans. We were having affairs with people we shared sleeping bags with.

We would be there for twenty-six days, almost a month.

We would change the course of history.

I didn't want to leave! I knew how important, how momentous the demonstration was. But I had a Rotary interview to attend, and I knew it could change my life – and the lives of other people with disabilities too.

What to do?

If you left the building, you could not come back. There was only one exception to this rule – if you performed a medical run and brought back supplies, you could re-enter. I volunteered.

I left the building early in the morning and picked up leg bags, catheters, and other personal hygiene supplies. I raced back to my apartment in Berkeley, where I showered and changed. Driving right on the speed limit, I got to my interview on time.

Before long I was seated among twenty men, all Rotarians, who seemed more interested in wheelchair sports than the problems of studying abroad. That was fine with me. It was kind of nice that they didn't doubt my ability to survive, and instead focused on basketball questions like "Exactly how tall is the basket?" (the same as for non wheelchair basketball players) and "What constitutes 'traveling'?" (taking more than two pushes without bouncing the ball).

Naturally, I kept it to myself that I was currently involved in the takeover of a federal building. I felt okay about the interview and, when it was over, raced back to the demonstration to hand over the medical supplies. Inside, folks were singing *We Shall Overcome* and *Keep Your Eyes on the Prize*, songs of the civil rights movement of African Americans. Rosa Parks, the famous black civil rights activist, was forced to sit at the back of a bus. Those of us with wheelchairs were not even allowed to *get on* the bus. Segregation and discrimination were beginning to crumble, but real progress would take many years.

When the 504 sit-in was over, I learned that I had received

the Rotary Scholarship to study in Australia. That would become part of a long journey, the genesis of an organization to bring disabled people from around the world to share ideas and strategies.

It was about our rights — to get on the bus, to go to a regular school, to go to university, to get a job, to get married, to become parents.

To live!

The power of the few

Decades after the 504 demonstration of 1977, I was fortunate to be able to tell the story of those watershed days to students, and to delegates from around the world.

They would watch video footage of those heady days when scores of disabled people and their non-disabled allies emerged triumphant from a federal government building, singing, shouting and fervently using sign language.

We were celebrating a new era.

People from around the world would watch in amazement. No one had ever learned of this historic event.

For several years I taught a course at the University of Oregon titled "Global Perspectives on Disability". Bright-eyed students, mostly non-disabled, would listen to the history of Section 504 with disbelief written all over their faces. Most students had assumed that the government of the United States of America had handed disabled people their rights on a platter.

After learning the history, they realized that if you want

change to happen, you can't wait for someone else. You need to make it happen yourself, joining with others and pursuing a common dream and passion. It's important to understand, as Paulo Freire wrote so powerfully, that an oppressed people cannot expect those who oppress to liberate them, but must liberate themselves with the assistance of trusted allies.

As Margaret Mead said, "Never doubt that a small group of thoughtful, committed citizens can change the world. Indeed, it is the only thing that ever has."

6.

What had I done? It was dark and rainy, and I was in a car with a man I didn't know. Brisbane looked awful, and I felt like I'd given up everything for it. Then a feeling of peace washed over me. Suddenly, I was amused by it all. I was at the beginning of a year-long adventure – a physical, spiritual and intellectual journey. Bring it on, I thought. Bring it on!

Ambassador of goodwill

I'd been sitting in a café in Berkeley when an advertisement in a student newspaper caught my eye.

"Study abroad. All expenses paid. Be an ambassador of goodwill."

Why not? I thought. *Sounds good to me!*

I followed up this scholarship opportunity and applied to my local Rotary Club. At the time I didn't really know what Rotary International was all about, and I didn't know how receptive the club would be to having someone in a wheelchair. I decided to go for it anyway. In order to be considered, I needed to complete some essays and pick a place to study.

Australia, I decided. It was far away, too expensive to get to on my own, and a place where English was spoken. Okay, there was another reason, too. I kind of liked the idea of seeing some wild kangaroos.

That's it, I thought. *Australia. I've got nothing to lose.*

Nothing to lose? In fact, I had a lot to lose. I was the co-director of the Berkeley Outreach Recreation Program. I had a great apartment a few blocks from campus that I shared with two women friends and an adorable French-Canadian guy who brought us warm chocolate chip cookies from the bakery he worked at each night. And there was Rod—a wonderful, loving boyfriend.

Why would I give all this up?

Journeying on alone

Rod and I had been on a wonderful journey together. We had jumped curbs and countless other obstacles together. We had crossed borders and pushed boundaries, limited only by our imagination.

Rod would find special travel packages in the newspaper. One of these enabled us to fly cheaply to Guatemala, Trinidad and New York during a winter break. We rode buses in Guatemala and swam in the turquoise waters of Trinidad.

Another time, as part of our studies, we were able to spend four months looking at recreation programs for people with disabilities in Europe. Somewhere near the Swiss Alps, we left our wheelchairs behind and rode sleds several miles down a slope before finding a train to take us back to the top of the mountain. We visited the Acropolis in Greece, asking two travelers from Canada to help us up the rocky incline, balancing our chairs on their rear wheels as if we were riding in wheelbarrows. Later that night we celebrated with our new-found friends in a little taverna, where everyone bought us retsina — the local wine. Why? Because our pictures had been taken for an Athens newspaper. People in wheelchairs on top of the Acropolis was big news, it seemed.

The same Canadian couple was game enough to follow us to Israel, where we achieved a similar feat by climbing Masada.

Life was great.

Perhaps it was even greater — more thrilling — because it wasn't easy. There were millions of flat tires. We were thrown out of restaurants in Paris because the owners claimed there was no room for wheelchairs. We were refused entry into museums because people were afraid we would break things, or because there were too many steps. Sometimes, we found the back entrances and the freight elevators, and went in anyway.

In England, they had huge wheelchair accessible bathrooms, the size of a small apartment — but you couldn't attend the theater without an able bodied chaperone.

I was incredulous. "Are you telling us we can't come into the National Theatre because we are both in wheelchairs and have no able bodied person with us?"

"Yes, I'm afraid that's so," said the matronly woman at the ticket counter. "It is against our policy to let you both come in unescorted. But with a chaperone you can get discounted tickets."

"You do realize that we are both adults, and have been traveling by ourselves for several months? This is the most ridiculous thing we have ever heard. This is blatant discrimination and would never be tolerated in the United States, where there are laws against this type of stupid behavior."

"Well, here in England we have fire laws governing safety. Perhaps you could come back with a chaperone? May I have the next person in line?"

"This is bullshit," Rod said. "Let's go. Let's get out of here."

"No."

I was furious and frustrated. Why should she win? Why should we go? I wanted to see the play. I was also eyeing a delicious piece of chocolate fudge cake displayed in the lobby café. I was not going to give up that easily.

I wheeled over to a young couple behind us in the queue to buy tickets and explained our predicament. They didn't seem particularly interested, but didn't object to helping us out. When their turn came, they casually asked for two tickets for themselves and two tickets for the discounted wheelchair seats. The ticket vendor was not amused, but realized we now had our "chaperones". Grim-faced, she put all four tickets on the counter. We reimbursed our accomplices, thanked them, and went our own way.

Later that week, we arrived to see *Macbeth* and were welcomed into the old, inaccessible theater by some young actors who literally had to drag us up two flights of stairs. It was the best Shakespeare play I had ever seen.

England was a land of paradoxes. Many public bathrooms were fully wheelchair accessible except for one thing — they were locked. A key could be obtained from an attendant in the non-accessible bathrooms. Going to a non-accessible bathroom — often up or down a flight of a stairs — to get a key for an accessible bathroom was enough to make you either laugh or cry.

Rod and I were a team. We'd embarked on the adventures

that we'd wanted to have before our accidents. We'd taken on the world, allowing nothing to deter us. Rod could read obscure maps and figure everything out, while I was an eternal optimist, prepared to ask anyone to do anything. At night he was my lover and made me feel beautiful and fulfilled.

It had been magical.

I knew, however, that I wanted the Rotary Scholarship to go to Australia — and that, if I got it, I'd be journeying on alone. I would leave everything familiar behind, knowing that I'd never return to my previous job or my quaint apartment.

I knew that I might also lose Rod if I left him for a year, but I needed to see what else was possible. I wanted to live by myself, on another continent, in another culture. I wanted to push some boundaries of my own.

When I heard that I'd been awarded the scholarship, I was thrilled. There was no turning back. What lay before me was one of the most exciting and challenging years of my life.

Brisbane

The man in the car was a Rotarian. I'd touched down in Brisbane, Australia, and he had been asked to collect me from the airport and take me to a residential college at the University of Queensland. The "ambassador of goodwill" had arrived.

The dormitory had installed grab bars to make its bathrooms more accessible for me. My vocational rehab counselor back in Berkeley had allocated funds to rent me a golf cart, just like the one I'd had in Berkeley, so I could get around the hilly campus easier with my wheelchair.

But that's where the similarities between Brisbane and Berkeley ended. Back in the late 1970s, Australians regarded Queensland as the "Far North" — an allusion to the USA's "Deep South". The government was dominated by rural conservatives and Brisbane, Queensland's capital, was a far cry from the much larger and more cosmopolitan cities of Sydney and Melbourne. I had come from the most progressive place, to study at one of least. While the Berkeley campus had hundreds of students with disabilities, I was now one of three students with disabilities — the other two being Aussie guys.

I was twenty five. I was in Australia, and I was on another adventure.

Like all exchange students taking a cross-cultural plunge, there were times when it was difficult, and times when it was exhilarating.

I needed to learn that going to someone's house for "tea" didn't really mean tea — it meant dinner. I needed to taste Vegemite — a blackish yeast extract used as sandwich spread — as a kind of initiation. I also needed to learn that people tended not to identify themselves with their professions. When you meet someone in the US, "What do you do?" is usually the next sentence after learning a person's name. At that time in Australia, that was a question that seemed to verge on rudeness. People identified themselves more with what they did in their leisure time — they had "barbies" (barbecues) with their friends, they watched cricket, or they played tennis. To compare occupations ran against the grain.

I missed my friends back home, so I hosted chocolate fondue parties in my room, realizing that I needed to take the initiative and make new friends. Slowly, people got to know me. I was a kind of celebrity being from the United States, but there were times when it wasn't easy being American. When NASA's Skylab crash landing in the Australian outback was dismissed by our president, many Australians were outraged, and it seemed that I was personally responsible for the incident. I was the Yankee. But I was also just Susan.

I had a distant cousin in Brisbane, who introduced me to two of his friends. They took me under their wings and whisked me away to beautiful beaches and forests on weekends. They indulged my American fantasies and took me to see kangaroos, koalas and platypuses. I was delighted.

Megan and Scott

I'd brought with me my expertise in organizing sports and recreation programs for disabled people, and I had also brought the Berkeley philosophy of merging academic life with a desire to "make a difference" in the real world. In Brisbane, I was surprised that most of the students at university — or "uni", as the Australians say — seemed to separate their study from life.

In one graduate course on the "normalization" of persons with disabilities, one student asked me: "Why do you keep asking so many questions? Don't you just want to know what is going to be in the exam?"

No thank you, I thought. I was there to learn, to ask questions and analyze. I didn't want to separate the examinable from the non-examinable, or theory from practice. I wanted the sum total.

Through one of my courses, I was able to develop an independent study looking at how children with spina bifida, aged between nine and twelve and attending mainstream schools, were affected by their level of participation in recreational activities. My hypothesis was that children who were active participants in recreational activities would have a more positive self-concept than those who did not actively participate—those who were spectators. I went to visit many homes of children with spina bifida, conducted extensive interviews with the children, and also spoke to their parents. What I found out made a profound impact on my work in later years.

Megan was a young girl with spina bifida who used a wheelchair. Her parents were outspoken in their desire for their daughter to have the same opportunities as other kids. Not surprisingly, their daughter felt the same way.

"So what do you do in school for recreation or physical education?" I asked.

"Nothing," she replied angrily. "All the other kids play softball or netball or volleyball, but I either have to keep score or go to the library. I want to play! I know I could, if someone just let me!"

I later asked Megan to complete the sentence, "I could be happy if…" She added: "… people would just give me the chance to try to do things like everyone else." I administered a tried and true self-concept evaluation test, and wasn't surprised when it indicated that she felt more positive than some of the other kids I tested.

Like Scott, for example. Scott had the same disability as Megan. When asked the same questions, he answered that he was happy keeping score or going to the library. He wasn't angry about that at all—he was resolved that it was his place in life. Scott's parents also seemed resolved. It was nice, they thought, that he could help the other kids, and that they were nice to him in return. When Scott was asked to complete the "I could be happy if…" sentence, he said: "… I could walk".

I remember thinking: barring miracles, this kid isn't going to be walking soon, or ever, so how can he ever be happy? Scott's acceptance of the role of a spectator in life, and his association of happiness with being "not disabled" was, to me, heartbreaking. A child, only nine years-old, had already resigned himself to a life without happiness. How tragic to think that, in Scott's world, the only real joy in life would be to get out of the wheelchair and start walking.

Who decided that?

I'd learned that there were countless other ways, and it disturbed me to think that children were being burdened with preconceived notions of what is important, and possible.

Why had disabled children and their families accepted such notions?

Just as importantly, what was I going to do about it?

Keys to happiness

When I arrived in Brisbane, I wanted to continue playing wheelchair basketball so I joined the local team.

It was no simple task. All the players were men, and a few of them were uncomfortable about letting me play. For a while, I needed to endure their glares and the disapproval of wives and girlfriends.

After a while, though, it was great. I quickly realized that there were many fine disabled athletes on the team, and we became buddies. I also realized that they could help me do something for children with disabilities. They could be role models.

My idea was to organize a Saturday morning sports club for disabled kids—to give them a chance to play sports instead of just watching them. I would have every sport possible, from basketball to archery to slalom courses for kids in manual and power wheelchairs. None of them would be made to keep the scores, and going to the library wouldn't even be an option.

No child would be left out. No child would be merely a spectator. No child would be unsuccessful.

I knew that this scheme would work best if the coaches were disabled adults—people they could identify with, so that they could begin to develop positive identities as well.

My new buddies on the wheelchair basketball team agreed to participate as coaches, and soon there were fifteen kids attending our Saturday morning sessions. Now, like their able bodied brothers and sisters, these kids had somewhere to go on the weekend to play sports. They were no longer watching from the sidelines. They were the stars.

From their parents, I started to hear that it was making a difference—not only to how the children saw themselves, but also to how their siblings and school friends saw them.

I learned something too. The experience supported my hypothesis about the value of active participation in recreational activities, and I was forever convinced that there needs to be a way to allow children with disabilities to be free from preconceived notions about what they can or cannot do. They themselves must make their own decisions about what is possible, and they need to know what those possibilities are.

It's wrong to believe that being non-disabled is the key to happiness. If there's a key for that particular door, the only one that's going to fit for people with disabilities is the one cut with an expectation of human rights and equal opportunities.

It's as simple — and as challenging — as that.

Where I am

As days rolled into months, there was a profound change in the way I felt about my life in Australia. At first, I had missed my friends, my food, my culture — but it wasn't long before I could read letters and cards from my friends in Berkeley without wishing I was back there with them.

I found myself thinking: *I want to be exactly where I am.*

I loved waking up in my ground floor dorm room and seeing the jacaranda trees outside, covered in mauve flowers. I loved the river that flowed around the university and through Brisbane itself. I loved the chorus of laughter of the kookaburra birds. I had come to enjoy the taste of Vegemite on toast and, when I needed a snack, I'd have a "bikkie" (biscuit, or cookie). I was also a fan of two popular Australian desserts, lamingtons and pavlova. I began using terms like "uni" (university) and "fair dinkum" — and I loved the way they sounded.

I had a sense of purpose, too. I felt as if I had made a difference by organizing sports for disabled teens, and it was fun playing basketball with the "blokes". The initial barriers had been broken down, and I'd learned an important lesson: Aussies "barrack" for their team instead of "rooting" for it. In Australia, to "root" means to have sex.

There were no ordinary days — each one seemed fresh and interesting. On weekends, I went to new places — a beautiful beach at Noosa, a picnic in the mountains of Katoomba.

I met a young guy who owned a Honda Goldwing 1000 motorcycle. Fearlessly, I accepted his offer to ride on the back of his bike up to Cairns, a place of tropical rainforests and spectacular coral reefs. The winding road hugged a magnificent shoreline. We passed fields of sugarcane and small, sleepy towns. I was on a journey where every moment held the promise of wonder.

Back in Brisbane, my friendships with people deepened. I felt less of a visitor, and more like I belonged.

Crush

Besides my studies, I soon had a crush on an architecture student I met while driving around the University of Queensland campus in my golf cart. His name was Peter, and he was beautiful. He had dark curly hair, a big smile, and strong body that looked like a surfer. I would give him a ride on my cart, and I started to hang out with some of his friends, who were progressive and interested in counterculture like people I'd known in Berkeley.

It was Andy the filmmaker all over again. I became obsessed with someone who, deep down, I knew was beyond my reach. Every time I saw him and we spoke, I felt myself falling into the grip of an infatuation.

The residential college held an annual prom—in Australia, it was called "the ball". Going to the ball was a very big deal and, to my own surprise, I really wanted to attend. I hadn't even gone to my own high school prom. The tragic war in Vietnam had weighed heavily on my graduating class and—with the support of teachers and administrators—we had decided against the frivolity of a prom and instead spent a day at the beach together.

But there I was, in Brisbane, getting caught up in prom frenzy. The only trouble was, I had no one to go with.

I could ask Peter, I thought. *But he wouldn't go with me… Would he?*

I thought it wouldn't hurt to ask, so I did. I dropped the question offhandedly, in my most nonchalant voice. He answered in the same fashion.

"Sure, why not?"

Oh, my goodness, he said yes. Suddenly I had to do all those things I had missed out on in high school—wear a long dress, set my hair, carefully apply some makeup. I was part of a preparation ritual that I had seen so many times in bad movies.

When Peter knocked on the door in his white tuxedo, I entered a world of fantasy. We got into one of the many chauffeured limousines that had lined up to transport the students to the ball. In light of all the alcohol that was to be consumed—some of it in fruity drinks that made it very easy to get "pissed", as they say in Australia—the limousines were not merely for show.

I was in heaven. Not only was Peter a drop-dead gorgeous guy who I'd thought was beyond my reach, he was also a fabulous dancer. I danced in my wheelchair and he hung on to my hand. We spun around and around — and, in my mind, dazzled everyone. When I looked into his eyes, the room blurred and it was as though no one else existed.

Of course I was also drinking the spiked fruit punch, which unfortunately caused me to take numerous trips to the bathroom — where transferring to a toilet with an ankle-length dress was no small task. But the punch had also made me tipsy and, if there was a happiness meter, I would have shattered it by going beyond all recorded measurements. I could see into Peter's eyes. We had finally connected.

Suddenly, around midnight, Peter suggested we go home, back to the dorm. The party looked certain to go on into the wee hours of the morning, so I was slightly disappointed and asked for one more dance, like Cinderella before her coach turned into a pumpkin. But I was not discouraged. What lay ahead?

The college was dark and quiet, and Peter walked me to my dorm room. I expected him to come in, and thought some kissing might ensue. Perhaps, too, we would go outside and find a nice place to sit in the warm breeze under the glow of the moon.

"I had a great time," Peter said, with his killer smile and radiant eyes.

God, he is gorgeous, I thought.

"I need to go now, and get my girlfriend and take her out to a party. Thanks again, it was fun."

With a quick peck on the cheek, he was gone.

I was crushed, devastated and in shock. In the weeks that followed, I wrote a song about Peter, which is more amazing than it sounds because I can't play an instrument or sing. I saw Peter occasionally on campus, but it stung. I continued to daydream about the impossible.

Then came the train ride.

I was on my way to Sydney, traveling on an overnight train by myself. Someone tapped me on the shoulder. To my complete disbelief, I looked up to see Peter. We talked for a while and it was easy. When the lights went out, a lot of the young travelers — many of them students — started making themselves comfortable on the floor of the aisle. Peter got out his sleeping bag and asked me if I wanted to share it with him.

We covered up, and suddenly I was kissing and holding Peter as the train rumbled south. It was a totally unexpected twist in the story of my mad crush. Our behavior was certainly unconventional for a train ride, but that wasn't going to stop me. It seemed like unfinished business.

I remember only disappointment. The fantasy evaporated. It was just a frolic in a sleeping bag with an attractive guy who thought I was fun. It wasn't such a big deal any more.

But I retained powerful memories of Peter and, many years later, found him on the Internet. He lived on an island in Torres Strait, helping Indigenous Australians win land rights. He swam with dolphins and surfed every day in the rough oceans. He had been married and divorced, and had three children from different women.

"Real relationships were never my thing," he told me. "I'm just not good at it."

I couldn't believe I had reconnected with him. We conversed a couple of times by email, but then my messages bounced back and he was lost again. In a strange way, I was relieved. The fantasy had always surpassed the reality.

Thirty years later, I would still remember one of the songs playing when Peter and I danced — *You took the words right out of my mouth*, by Meatloaf. Whenever I heard it, I would still feel the excitement and trepidation of that night with Peter. Why *is* that? Why is the fantasy and romance of being with someone you think you can't have, someone beyond your grasp, so compelling?

7.

I grabbed my two canes and headed out of the bus toward Ayers Rock. I didn't have a plan. All I knew was that I hadn't come all this way to sit tight and wait for everyone else to come back, fulfilled and animated by their adventure.

Hitchhiking in New Zealand

We'd been sitting by the road for an hour — maybe more. No one had even slowed down. If we got lucky, we'd soon be heading for a place with a name I wasn't sure how to spell, and hadn't even heard of just a short time ago.

Rod was getting frustrated and I heard him muttering under his breath. "We could be here for days," he said, blowing a light mist into the chill air.

It was a break between semesters — winter in the southern hemisphere. Rod had decided to visit me and we'd set out for New Zealand. The old team reunited, we were once again heading off the beaten track. No package tours for us! All we had was a loose plan to hitchhike around and experience both islands. It never crossed our minds that this was a bit unusual for two people in wheelchairs. For us, it was just what young travelers did.

But no one was picking us up. Our backpacks were attached

to the back of our wheelchairs. We had smaller packs under our wheelchairs, which provided balance and supplies for the day. When cars appeared, we would stick out our thumbs, but no one seemed to notice. Well, they noticed, I guess. They must have. They gave us puzzled looks and then drove on by.

Maybe, I thought, it was time to change tactics.

"We should make a sign or something and hold it up, just to make sure they know we are actually heading somewhere. How about we try that?"

My thoughts were confirmed when the next car came by, and an elderly woman smiled and waved like we were cute kids playing by the side of the road. Yup, we definitely needed to change tactics.

We tore out some paper from Rod's notebook.

"Is it 'Timuru' or 'Timaru'?"

Neither of us was certain, but I wrote "Timaru" in big letters as the name of our next destination. This seemed to help, as cars now began to slow down to read the sign.

Still no one stopped. It was getting dark and I was beginning to wonder if Rod was right—we'd be stuck there for days. I had a new idea.

"Go up the road a little and hide behind that tree," I said.

"What?"

Rod wasn't impressed. In fact, he was downright annoyed by my suggestion. But he knew that we were running out of time. It would start to go dark soon, and hitchhiking would be practically impossible. He was willing to try whatever I dreamed up.

With Rod out of sight, I sat in my wheelchair and smiled meekly with my handwritten sign. I stuck out my thumb and invisibly crossed my fingers. Amazingly, within minutes, a car slowed down. A man in his thirties wound down a window.

"What are you doing?" His voice was low, quizzical.

"I'm hitchhiking to Timaru," I told him with a big smile.

"So how am I going to get your wheelchair in my boot?"

By now I have learned that "boot" means "trunk" in Australia. "The wheels pop off," I told him. "It will fit in easily."

As soon as I was in the back seat with my chair stowed in the boot, I tried to slip in that my travel partner was just up the road.

"Oh," said the driver with a deep chuckle. "No worries."

"And he's in a wheelchair, too." I said this sweetly, trying to be casual, but my voice had a whiny, begging tone to it. Fortunately, the man still found it quite amusing.

"Does your friend have another friend hiding a little further on?" He laughed heartily. "And another one after that? All in wheelchairs?"

Rod emerged from behind his tree as the car slowly turned the corner.

"Getting two wheelchairs in the boot is going to be interesting," the driver said.

"It will be okay. I even have a bungee cord in case the boot won't close properly."

Once Rod was in the car, the man asked us about our travels and was amazed at our plan to hitchhike for six weeks. He invited us to his home for dinner, and offered us a place to sleep the night. Rod figured out a way to use the "inaccessible" bathroom by strapping a belt around his chair, making it narrow enough to squeeze through the door. We enjoyed a beautiful meal and met our rescuer's wife and kids. By the end of the night, he had called his friends and relatives all over New Zealand, and a whole network of people had offered to pick us up in different cities, feed us and let us stay in their homes. What an amazing country.

When we didn't have rides organized, we went back to our winning formula for hitchhiking, using signs and hiding Rod behind a bush or tree when necessary. We rode in huge trucks—or "lorries", as they call them—through high mountain passes, perched high next to the driver with wide window panes that overlooked lush valleys and dazzling lakes. Portly men secured our wheelchairs to the truck with a few bungee cords, and they rattled outside in the fresh breeze.

I was blissfully happy. I loved sitting by the side of the road, reading a great novel while basking in the sun, never knowing what adventure lay ahead of me. We visited snow-covered glaciers and the steaming and bubbling springs of Rotorua. We bought hand-knitted wool sweaters in white and gray to remind us of the sheep grazing on rolling green hills. We shared stories with numerous families from all over the country.

Looking back at photographs from that time, I would see a cherub, my face and breasts made full and round from drinking the cream that plugged the necks of home-delivered milk bottles. My face expressed wonder. I was letting fate play its hand, trusting in the next car, the next encounter. For me, it wasn't hitchhiking in a wheelchair that was amazing—it was the lives that were touched, the providence of moments that connect people, sometimes planned, sometimes by chance.

There was the funny and hyperactive Hershey executive whose house was filled with more chocolate than anyone could possibly consume. He was married to a quiet vegetarian yoga disciple, who didn't eat sugar and spent hours meditating and doing intricate yoga exercises. *Opposites attract*, I thought. Evenings were never boring as Rod and I glimpsed into the everyday lives of so many families.

Anne and Pete were among a number of couples who picked us up. Pete had received a call from a friend of his, asking him to go and collect us in Oamaru. The friend didn't tell him about our wheelchairs, so Pete had grabbed his kids and hopped into his Volkswagen Golf. Somehow, he managed to fit us in. Anne and Pete said they admired our "zany and courageous attitude". We shared picnics in the park, and I remember being amazed that Anne cooked and froze mulligatawny soup so that she could always be prepared for instant dinners and fabulous picnics. The mind is a strange and magnificent sieve that allows some moments and details to become embedded in our consciousness while thousands of other grains of memory slip through to nowhere. Why the mulligatawny soup remained with me is a mystery.

Years later, Anne and Pete visited my parents' home in New York. My mom and dad returned their hospitality, giving them a whirlwind tour of Manhattan. They were introduced to bagels, lox and cream cheese, which they have since enjoyed while thinking of my folks. I learned of conversations they'd had with Dad about his experiences during the Holocaust, and was reminded that intimate conversations reveal the closeness of brief acquaintances.

Hitchhiking in New Zealand—"Land of the Long White Cloud". After a semester of study in Australia, I had needed a break, and it had proven to be a magical time. It was an adventure that would be difficult to repeat today, with the world no longer as safe and innocent as it was then. Only once in a six-week adventure did I feel scared, and that was only because a man drove too fast.

The journey reminded me of the miracle of travel, and what it teaches us about life. The unexpected, the unplanned, the hospitality of strangers. It brought me back to the thoughts I'd had years earlier: *Capture these moments, these relationships, these magical sequences of events. Remember the laughter, the happiness, the sorrow. Cherish them.*

Perhaps that is some sort of life force, too rarely heard.

This is life, it whispers. *Treasure it. It will be gone soon.*

Inner voices

I am living in Australia. Quite often, I needed to remind myself of this. It felt like home.

Where *was* home, anyway? I was no longer sure. Years had passed since I lived in New York, and Berkeley was home while I was studying and establishing BORP. But I'd graduated, and left my employment in Berkeley, and I was uncertain about what I'd go back to there. Should I go somewhere new? Where?

Maybe I belonged right where I was, in Brisbane. That inner voice started whispering to me, telling me that I didn't want the year to end.

There was a man on the basketball team who wanted me to stay. Like Rod, Fred was divorced from a woman who couldn't adjust to life with a husband in a wheelchair. Fred knew about Rod, but he also knew that Rod was from my other life, and we didn't talk about it much. Rod and I had been very honest with each other in New Zealand, and he'd told me that he'd been with someone else. I hadn't expected anything else. A year is a long time to be away.

Fred had become my boyfriend—unlike Peter, a "real" boyfriend. He drove me to the interviews I conducted in the homes of teens with spina bifida. On weekends, he took me out on his boat. We'd go to idyllic places like Byron Bay, a cove with the bluest of waters.

"Susan, you could stay here," Fred would say. "You don't have to go back to the United States. I would rent a house for you here in Byron Bay in the summer and come up on weekends, if you like. Why do you have to go?"

Had I fallen in love with Fred?

No, but perhaps I had fallen in love with Australia, and with the life it offered me.

I felt alive, aware and proud of my uniqueness.

Exploring the outback

During my second semester at the University of Queensland, I got to have a few weeks off. What to do?

I'd heard a lot about the "outback" and Ayers Rock, a giant monolith right in the centre of Australia that is sacred to Indigenous people. I'd also heard of the Olgas, a massive outcrop of rock not far to Ayers Rock's south. I wanted to explore these places, and discovered that there was a thirty-day camping tour that did just that. It sounded like fun. Naively, I signed up.

For days—it seems like weeks—the bus drove over flat, dry

desert land while a core of the younger folks sat at the back, making out. I sat by myself, face pressed to a window in the outback of Australia, and felt as lonely as I had ever been.

I was the only crip. That wouldn't have been so bad, but it seemed like none of the boisterous Aussie teens on the bus had even talked to a crip before. They'd never had to, and they didn't care to. The bus rattled on over the vast outback. There was laughing and singing and, for a while, even a makeshift bowling alley down the center aisle of the bus, with Coke bottles being skittled by an orange. People were doing anything to pass the time.

We visited Cooper Pedy, a small town built underground that mined opals. Imagine living underground to stay cool! We went to Mataranka, an oasis of lush green plants like a tropical mirage in the midst of a parched desert. Away from the teens, I used these interludes to talk to local people and any other travelers I could find. I made friends with a man who was making a grueling, continent-wide trek on a camel.

Every night we set up camp, erected our tents and waited for dinner. At times, there were so many flies on my face and arms that I could hardly see. They were relentless. If I was pushing my wheelchair or standing with my canes I had no way of brushing them off my face, so they settled down to picnic until I shook my head like a hot and bothered horse. I found myself wishing I had a tail.

Then, of course, it was back on the bus for us all—many flies included.

During long days on the hot stuffy bus, I prayed that I wouldn't have to pee. That would *really* have tipped everyone over the edge with me. I tried not to drink a lot, but it was thirsty weather.

Was it fun? No. But I was doing what I wanted to do—getting beyond the cities of Brisbane and Sydney to the famous "outback". I wanted to remember everything. The best of times and the worst of times—I reminded myself to embrace them both.

That was more than I could do at a small bar in the middle of nowhere, with a bartender who wanted a cheap laugh from his customers. Sick of sugary cans of drink and yearning for something more refreshing, I waited my turn to be served.

"Do you have any juice here?"

The bartender answered me with his voice raised, so that everybody could see what a funny man he was. "Do we have any *Jews* here? I bloody well hope not!"

I was mortified. People laughed. How did I respond?

How *did* I respond?

I'm not even sure. As years pass, my brain filtered the detail and I could only be certain of my shock and anger.

Part of me remembered saying, "No, I said *juice!*"

According to my father, though, I returned from Australia and told him another version of the story. In that version, I told the obnoxious bartender that I wanted fruit juice – and that *yes,* there *was* a Jew in the bar, and it was *me.*

When my dad said that, I hoped his memory was better than mine.

Climbing a monolith

We were drawing close to Ayers Rock, and everybody on the bus was excited. Anticipation had been building and, when we finally arrived, all the other passengers rushed off without even giving me a glance. The bus driver told me to wait where I was.

You have got to be kidding, I thought.

I started moving toward the front of the bus.

"I don't know where you're going, but we won't wait for you," the driver said. He was clearly annoyed, but I didn't care. Grabbing my canes, I got off the bus. There was no way I was going to sit tight and wait for everyone else to come back.

It takes most non-disabled people a few hours to climb this huge, steep rock, which is almost like a mountain. There was no point dragging my wheelchair out of the luggage compartment because the ground underfoot was gravel, several inches deep, which would have immobilized me completely. I drove my canes into the gravel and wobbled my way to the base of the rock. It was hot, and I had a cold, making my heart beat a little faster than normal.

After taking one step up, I could see that my task was impossible. I'd never be able to walk up Ayers Rock unassisted. I sat down. The peak of the mountain was behind me, and I began to inch myself up on my butt.

It was the only way.

With my knees bent, and using the strength of my arms, I was able to cover about a foot at a time. The sun was beating down and the rock was orange red. After an hour of climbing—like a snail going backwards—the buses below were like small toys, with tourists scattered around them like ants.

I was filthy with red dirt. My nose was running, and my heart was pounding. I might have had a fever but I didn't care.

Look here, fools! Hey, you asshole bus driver! Look here! I am near the top of Ayers Rock and you thought I couldn't do it.

Okay, I didn't quite make it to the top, but I was nevertheless victorious. As I began to descend, I felt both peaceful and exhilarated. I returned to the bus, still pretty much ignored by the rest of the group. There had been another tour bus, air conditioned with older folks doing the same trip. Momentarily, I wished I'd taken that bus instead—but I rejected the thought because it threatened to spoil my moment of triumph.

My eyes scanned the horizon. There was a beautiful sunset, an orange and magenta sky.

How cool! I thought.

At the time, I believed that my elation was all about having climbed Ayers Rock, which was later returned to Indigenous Australians to become known as Uluru. Years later, I would come to know that my victory back then was even bigger than it seemed.

Didgeridoo

Thirty days can be a long time. On that bus, I observed shifts in relationships—some subtle, some not so subtle. Small talk ran to a trickle. People got bored, tired or amorous. Some read books. Some became irritable. Many retreated into silence. A few of the "blokes" on the bus got restless, the confined space unable to contain them. When they became bored with their snooty girlfriends, they began chatting with me. We exchanged stories. The trip became more tolerable.

Okay, I'll admit it. I was starting to have fun. On a trip like that, a little conversation makes all the difference. As the trip entered its final week, I was starting to feel giddy with a sense of accomplishment. But perhaps the most memorable episode in my exploration of the outback was yet to come.

We arrived at the Olgas. Outside the bus window, jagged red rocks emerged from a barren desert. There were tall trees with bright green foliage, and the sky was deep blue. The sun was piercing. As usual, everyone raced off the bus, leaving me to fend for myself. Reluctantly, the bus driver opened the storage compartment beneath the bus and yanked out my wheelchair. He made this seem as though it was the world's most difficult task. It was his job.

"Where do you think you are going?"

He couldn't have sounded meaner or more arrogant if he tried. It was déjà vu, Ayers Rock all over. Again he had me thinking *asshole*, but it just wasn't worth arguing with the guy. At that point, I didn't really care what he thought. I was going to be so glad to get rid of him in a couple more days.

He kept on. "It's all gravel—the whole way to the canyon. We'll only be here for two and a half hours, and you can't even push one meter in this stuff. I'm just telling you now, we won't wait for you." He took out his cigarettes, lit up and walked away.

He was right about the gravel. I couldn't push at all, and immediately got stuck. Hot, thirsty, frustrated—and stuck. I was also ready to kill the bus driver, along with all the other people on the bus for leaving me alone.

Fuck them, I thought. *I'm going.*

Going where? Who am I kidding?

I didn't care. I was going *somewhere*. I took my canes and

moved very slowly, leaving my wheelchair behind. I walked shakily and almost fell several times on terrain that was loose with jagged rocks. I was getting nowhere fast.

There was a burning sensation in my thighs—a signal that I just couldn't take another step. A small tree offered the only shade around, and I dragged myself toward it. I fell to the ground when my legs gave out.

It was a disaster. Unmitigated. I would bake in the sun for the next two and a half hours while everyone else had a fabulous time at one of Australia's natural wonders. The bus driver would not look for me. Luckily, I didn't think about snakes and spiders and the thousands of insects that would welcome the novel taste of an immobilized New Yorker.

I wasn't scared. I wasn't depressed. I was in a bad adventure and I didn't know how it would turn out. There was no possibility of walking back to the bus and I had no idea what would happen to me. In a bizarre kind of way, I was amused. There was a wry smile on my face.

You've really done it this time, Susan!

I sat and waited.

Then, out from behind some faraway bushes, a man appeared. He was walking toward me. He was handsome and strong, wearing dark sunglasses and khaki shorts with an olive shirt showing off his muscular arms. His leg muscles bulged.

I must be hallucinating. It's the heat. I've been warned about sunstroke.

The man was grinning at me. Even accounting for the glare, his teeth were dazzling. The look on his face was almost as if he'd been searching for me his whole life.

Maybe I fainted. Maybe I hit my head on the rocks. Surely this isn't real?

"G'day," he said, kneeling down beside me. "Are you okay?"

"Well…"

I told him the whole story. My outback trip… the obnoxious bus driver… the helpful folk on the bus who abandoned me.

"No worries, mate!"

He asked my permission to pick me up. I gave it, perhaps more willingly than I would in other circumstances. He picked me up and carried me piggy back style and I felt the solid warmth of his body under a shirt damp with sweat.

"Off we go," he said. He walked briskly, and I hung on in utter disbelief.

We walked for hours. We walked over rocks and streams and through the miraculous gorge of the Olgas. When we rested, I sat beside him and he told me about the land, the history.

He was a bus driver. His tour group had gone exploring for a few hours, so he was happy to spend time with me. We ran into a friend of his — an old Aboriginal man who gave me a beautiful didgeridoo he'd made.

The thought that I was out of my mind with sunstroke wouldn't go away, but I decided to enjoy it anyway. These were magic moments. All my struggles, all the unpleasantness — all worth it. The magnificent Olgas would be imprinted in my memory forever.

Eventually we approached the bus. I was beaming as my Olive Oyl body bounced around on his broad back. He was grinning too, still walking at a rapid pace. My God he was fit!

All the other people in my group were on the bus already. I got that *I can't believe you made us wait* look and the driver growled: "You're late, hurry up!"

I gave my savior a big hug, almost tearful with gratitude. By the tenderness of his embrace, I knew he understood what he had done for me.

A quarter of a century later, a didgeridoo hangs in my room. It's a constant reminder of that day.

Trust.

Expect the unexpected.

Brushes with officialdom

"Telephone call for you, Susan."

There was only one phone at the end of the hall in the residential college I lived in at the University of Queensland. Whenever it rang, the person nearest answered and it was their job to find the person requested. If you happened to be around, you got the call.

"I'm coming," I yelled from my room, dashing down the hall wondering who it might be.

The voice on the phone was that of an older man. "Susan Sygall?"

He was Australian, serious and sounded official.

"When are you leaving Australia? Do you have your ticket yet? You do understand that your visa will expire soon, and that you are obliged to leave, don't you?"

I explained to this man, as I'd explained to immigration

officials when I first arrived, that I was in Australia on a full scholarship from Rotary International. "Yes," I told him. "I am going home when my scholarship expires and I have completed my studies here."

Thank you so much, and goodbye!

What were they so worried about? They appeared to be assuming that, because I was disabled, there was a high chance that I would stay in the country and "bludge on the dole" — live on welfare.

Give me a break! I would think. *I have spent most of my life in school and university to have a fabulous career... How dare they make that assumption!*

Were they calling all Rotary Scholars, or just the one in the wheelchair? This is the treatment that disabled people tend to get everywhere, including those coming to the United States. Immigration officials assume that our one aim in life is to become a welfare statistic.

One day, the phone at the end of the hall rang for me again. Was it the Department of Immigration again, reminding me that my visa was going to expire, asking when I would leave?

"Are you Susan Sygall?"

"Yes, I am."

"I've heard so much about you, about the wonderful programs you have organized for disabled teenagers. Would you be interested in a job as a recreation therapist here in Brisbane? We think we may have a position for you."

"Really?" I was stunned.

A thought occurred to me: maybe this *was* my home now, maybe I didn't have to go back to the States? I had good friends, and I could have a job. Beyond that year in Brisbane, I really had no plans. Nothing was set in stone.

I took a few days to think about it and spent most of that time thinking that the year had been like a dream, and how wonderful it was that it didn't have to end. No longer would I need to say goodbye in a few weeks' time. I had learned that Australia is a vast and beautiful country – from the brilliant colors of the reefs I snorkeled at Heron Island, to the tropics of Darwin and cosmopolitan Sydney with its breathtaking opera house. The friends I had made were real, more real than the letters from Berkeley and New York. Those lives now seemed distant from my own.

I thought, I pondered. I was between two worlds.

Then I realized that I had made a commitment to Rotary International. I had been given a generous scholarship, based on a promise to be an ambassador of goodwill and visit Rotary clubs throughout Australia, and then to finish my studies in the US and share what I had learned and accomplished. I had fulfilled the first half of my obligations, but not the second. I needed to honor the agreement.

I also needed to think about my mom and dad. They had flown around the world to visit me in Australia, but expected me to come home when my year was done. I did miss them. I was very far away. The same applied to Rod. Despite our separate "wanderings", we had remained close and shared a wonderful time in New Zealand.

Immigration officials in Australia could heave a sigh of relief. I loved Australia, but would go home.

8.

I boarded a plane for Oregon. The door closed and an elegant flight attendant walked along the aisle, clicking down overhead baggage hatches. I was sad that the most exhilarating part of my life, where each day was unexpected and surprising, was coming to a close.

What next?

Phone calls from Australian immigration served one useful purpose. They made me face up to the need for a decision about my future. It had been scary enough facing up to leaving a place that now felt like home, but it was even scarier contemplating decisions about what to do next.

What was my destination?

Would it be another temporary one, or should I be thinking longer term?

I would not return to Berkeley. I had said goodbye to that chapter of my life, and I was not one for going backwards. New York teemed with opportunities, but it also teemed with memories. I'd moved on.

The truth was, I had nowhere to go. I needed a plan.

My good friend Diane had received a scholarship to get a

Master's degree in therapeutic recreation from the University of Oregon. Diane and I had so much in common, from childhood in New York to our separate experiences of Colorado, and then as co-founders of the Berkeley Outreach Recreation Program (BORP). Hearing that I was uncertain about what to do after my Rotary year, Diane suggested that I apply for a scholarship to finish my own Master's degree in Eugene. There was even a studio apartment available near where she lived.

Eugene, Oregon?

I had never imagined living in Oregon—I hadn't even been there.

There was nothing to lose. Diane's suggestion made sense. I filled out the University of Oregon application forms, investigated scholarship possibilities in the therapeutic recreation program, and waited.

Moira

Moira was a slight, modest and academically brilliant woman of about my own age. She came from Nova Scotia, Canada, and as postgraduate students living in the same residential college in Brisbane we had shared many bulk-cooked meals. I liked her dancing brown eyes and ready smile. We'd each had highs and lows, and had become friends.

Moira's scholarship year was also coming to an end. Like me, she was beginning to come to terms with the thought of going home. To be honest, we were starting to depress ourselves, talking about the friends and places we would miss in Australia. For two very optimistic people, it was weird.

I wanted to lighten the mood. "Well," I said. "If we do have to go home soon, let's do something really crazy and fun."

"Like what?" Moira threw me a mischievous glance, and it told me that she was up for anything.

"Let's go travel through Asia. We can go home the long way — there are heaps of places out there that are a lot closer to Australia than they are to the States, or to Nova Scotia."

"Wow," said Moira. "That would be wild, but I don't have much money to spend."

"Neither do I! But there must be a cheap way of doing it."

I was getting excited already — starting to think about a whole new adventure instead of dwelling on the one that was about to end.

At the student travel office, we discovered that the cheapest way was to take local buses through Indonesia, Malaysia and Thailand, with a few cheap flights to get us to Bali and Singapore. Somehow, we would end up in London, where we could take our own flights home.

Moira was nonchalant about the fact that she would need to *shlep* (carry) my wheelchair up and down more places that she could ever imagine. The truth was, we were both so giddy about the whole idea that we weren't even thinking straight. If either of us had really known what we were getting ourselves into, we might have run out of that travel office as fast as we could.

Luckily, we had no idea. We launched ourselves into an unforgettable adventure. Sometimes, not knowing can be a blessing.

Trading places

Moira and I were full of wonder as we meandered around the backstreets of Jogjakarta, Indonesia. Beautiful handmade batiks hung at the front of little stores, swaying in the warm breeze. The evening was filled with enchanting gamelan music.

For many of the locals, however, I was a source of equal wonder. I became the center of attention wherever I went, with small crowds watching my every move. Eventually the staring which many travelers experience in Asia began to wear on me, especially since the stares were not merely curious, but carried more than a hint of disgust. Despite having acquired so much self-confidence and pride, being treated that way was more than I could take.

While visiting a small museum, I confided in Moira. "I can't stand all these people staring at me and following me around like I'm some sort of circus freak. I need a break."

We were talking in a corridor away from the crowds, near the toilets, where few people were around. Even so, people waiting near the bathrooms began to form a small circle around me, staring at my wheelchair.

Moira looked at me quizzically. She knew I had something in mind.

"I'm not sure how much more I can take right now. I just need a break. Why don't you get in my chair for a while?"

"Sure," Moira replied. "Why not?" She would have done anything to put me out of my anguish for at least a while.

I sat on the steps, and lost myself in a novel. I also lost the feeling of being under the public microscope, and cherished a few moments of being perceived as a normal person.

And although it makes no sense, the same people who had watched Moira get into my wheelchair followed her out into the main part of the museum. A crowd gathered around her, and stared at her as she wheeled herself around the beautiful sculptures and ancient relics.

Trading places was weird — but good for both of us. We experienced another reality.

After a good night's sleep, and a few days spent on beautiful white beaches, my love for travel resurfaced. Friendships formed in small shops where we bought carved wooden salad bowls, which would forever remind me of our journey.

I began winking at the people who stared at me — which caused them to either flee or to smile at me, breaking down the barrier that had so isolated me at first.

Ferry to anywhere

Perhaps the scariest part of our five-week odyssey came during our time in Malaysia. It began when an older, affluent-looking and slightly overweight man started talking to Moira, befriending her. We were getting a little worn down, and welcomed social contact from one of the locals. When the man suggested taking us to dinner at an expensive restaurant we naively agreed, without questioning his motives.

The restaurant was beautiful and the food was fabulous — a world away from our low-budget travelers' fare, which mainly consisted of noodles and bananas. After a while, however, Moira started giving me strange looks. Her eyes kept darting down to her lap as if trying to alert me to something. Finally, I understood. I dropped my napkin and, when I leaned down, saw the man's hand on Moira's knee. She put it firmly back on his own leg, but he replaced it immediately—this time on her thigh.

Had we been older and more experienced, we might have just gotten up and left. But this man had been drinking a lot of wine, and we had just consumed an expensive meal we had no way of paying for.

To make things worse, he seemed to know everyone in the restaurant. For all we knew, he might have known everyone in the whole town, or even been the chief of police. We sensed that we wouldn't be getting much support from those around us.

"I'm really tired Moira," I said. "I think we should head back to our hotel."

I was trying to sound confident. The truth was that we didn't actually *have* a hotel. In our usual free and easy way, we were going to think about backpacker accommodation later. We didn't even know where any hotels were located.

"Yeah, I'm tired too," Moira replied. We both knew we needed to extricate ourselves from the situation as soon as possible. "Thank you so much for the lovely dinner."

"Not so fast," the inebriated man replied. "I have arranged for you ladies to stay in a beautiful hotel room." He pointed out the window to a fancy high rise building a few blocks away.

"Oh that's so kind, but we already have a room," Moira replied. I had never seen her lie through her teeth before.

"No, I insist you stay in this room I have rented for you, near my room." The man spoke sternly, as if he thought we were playing some coy game and wanted to end it.

Panic began to show our eyes. What to do?

This wasn't funny, or exciting. We were scared—real scared.

"I'll be right back," he said motioning that he was going to the bathroom. You can't drink as much wine as he'd been drinking without nature calling, and it suddenly seemed that nature might be our savior.

The man looked Moira directly in the eye. "Don't go away."

As soon as he was out of sight, we were out of there. We made a dash for the door and I pushed my wheelchair hard on to the busy street. There simply wasn't time to go up and down the inaccessible curbs, so the madness of the traffic was my only alternative. Moira bravely followed. Thanks to the rickshaws, my chair wasn't the only vehicle without an engine, and we made good progress. Finally, we ended up in a side street and saw a place that seemed to have rooms to rent. We went straight in and paid whatever price they asked. No bartering now—we were paying for our safety.

Moira was terrified. "He's going to be so furious that he'll look for us and use his contacts to find us. Someone will tell him where we are—it's not as though we exactly blend into the crowd."

"Maybe, but we can't go back outside now, so let's sit tight for a while."

Neither of us slept a wink. Every creak in that old building put us into a panic. It wasn't even 4.00 a.m. when we decided to take our chances.

"Let's get out of here," I said to Moira. "We'll go straight to the ferries and just get the hell out of here."

Quietly we packed our things.

In the dim light, we raced across town to the waterfront and jumped on a ferry to anywhere, leaving our naivety, and some of our innocence, behind.

Family

Somewhere in the middle of our journey, in some small dusty village, I was moved by the sight of a small boy. Our encounter lasted no more than a few seconds but changed my life.

Moira and I were going to a marketplace to buy some bananas. Dirt roads were plied by undernourished donkeys with sad eyes. My arms were tired from pushing over the bumps and gravel in my wheelchair. I was wearing sports gloves, like the ones used for handball, which left my fingers free to open my backpack or peel some fruit. The gloves also protected me from the horse, donkey and cow dung that littered the street and was picked up by my wheels.

As we entered the open air market, I caught the brown eyes of a young, thin boy. No more than twelve years old, he was sitting in a torn rag on the dirt floor. His legs were twisted and atrophied, and his elbows seemed locked, his arms striking forward with fists clenched. It was obvious that he couldn't control these sudden jolts. There was a paltry array of coins in a bowl in front of him, thrown in by other villagers who pitied him, or perhaps as a kind of prayer that their own families would not be touched by such misfortune.

I recognized all the signs of cerebral palsy.

Our eyes locked on each other.

The boy stared at my bright purple, expensive-looking

sports wheelchair, perhaps wondering what planet I came from and how I arrived in his tiny village.

For me, it was as though time slowed down, and everyone had disappeared but the two of us. We just stared at each other. His eyes seemed to light up and dance with amazement. I didn't feel sorry for him, or look at him in disgust like so many others who passed by.

A single concept, expressed by a single word, filled my head — like some ancient revelation.

Family.

He was family.

I looked at him and connected with him somewhere deep inside. I understood the connection immediately, and knew that it transcended cultures and borders. It was a connection I didn't feel with other people — not with Moira, nor with the majority of my friends in the United States and Australia.

This boy and I were vastly different. We were from different worlds. But we shared a common experience and it was profound. I couldn't describe it, nor explain it.

Family.

And then it was as though the spell was broken, and the moment was gone. I turned a corner. Someone dropped a coin into his bowl, and I looked for Moira among mountains of bananas.

This notion of an extended family, however, lodged in my soul. Something had changed for me — forever.

The buses of Thailand

We arrived in Bangkok. It was incredibly noisy, dusty and hot. There were traffic jams and honking cars everywhere.

We hadn't realized how hard it would be to take local buses. They were already filled with more people than the bus should carry, and we could barely fit inside.

There was a routine we learned to follow — it was the only way. I would lean forward and grab the handrails at the entrance to the bus. Then, I'd sit on my rear end and haul myself up the stairs, one step at a time. When I reached the top, I would crawl to a seat or — since the buses were so crowded — claim a piece of the floor. Moira's small but strong body would lug my wheelchair up behind me. More often than not, no one helped her. They'd just stare at the two of us in disbelief.

But we were determined and didn't let any of this get us down. We took buses to places like Borobudur, where a giant Buddha sat peacefully in gardens at the outskirts of Bangkok. In the more touristy places, where there were more young travelers like us from around the world, we'd find instant friends from Germany or Sweden to give us a hand while we exchanged travel highlights and nightmares. Even on our meager budget we could find small restaurants and sample a variety of coconut shakes, tropical fruits, spicy noodles and peanut sauce. Such delights made all the hassles of travel just melt away.

But sticking to the beaten tourist track was never our plan. We held a booklet of over thirty ticket stubs — our prepaid right of access to buses that left from tiny villages in the middle of the night and went to places we couldn't pronounce. There were no other tourists or hippie-looking travelers on those buses. No one spoke English, and how we managed to get on to the *right* buses would always remain a mystery to me.

We were stared at constantly. Small children touched my motionless legs and laughed, as though they were two strange creatures in hibernation. Sometimes parents yanked their children away from me, fearful that they might catch whatever evil ailment had brought my body to its destiny of shame. Occasionally, there was the sweet smile of an old man. A toothless smile, beaming from a creased, sunburned face, had the power to make me believe once again in the beauty and humanity of people who do not fear that which is different from themselves.

Traveling on Thailand's buses made some of life's basic necessities a little difficult — to say the least. We stopped in the middle of nowhere, often in the middle of the night, usually near a place where vendors were cooking unidentifiable food on small grills by candlelight. We searched for something resembling a bathroom — usually a cement stall with a hole in the floor that people could squat over.

The smell was awful. It was so pungent that I breathed into my shirt to avoid throwing up. Of course, squatting to pee was beyond me. I managed to maneuver my body so that I was a few inches off the edge of my wheelchair cushion, and tried to get lined up with the hole in the floor. Above all, I didn't want to wet my shoes, or the backpack under my chair. My method wasn't pretty — but it worked.

Sometimes Moira and I stayed overnight in hostel-type accommodations, usually cement rooms, costing the equivalent of about seventy-five cents a night. The bathroom was often impossible, either because I couldn't get to the hole on the floor, or because the smell was just too repugnant. In those situations I performed my "hanging over the seat of my wheelchair" act, using a wide-mouthed bottle to catch the urine. I often needed to pee near my bed in the dark, as I'd have needed an extra hand to hold a flashlight. One night, I peed into the bottle and became a bit frantic when, unexpectedly, my urine kept coming and coming, full stream. The bottle filled and I felt the warm overflow, dribbling down my hands and forming a puddle on the floor. Soon it turned into a river, headed toward Moira's bed. I could have cried—but instead I burst out laughing at the absurdity of it all.

"Hey Moira, wake up! You are not going to believe this…"

Next morning, I cleaned the floor and myself as best as I could with a damp cloth, and we resumed our adventures with buses.

Some time later, we took a bus at dusk. The driver lit a small stick of incense, and someone who spoke a small amount of English told us that this would ensure our safe passage over dark, winding roads through the mountains.

I was soon hoping it was very powerful incense because our driver turned out to be a lunatic. His foot rode the accelerator heavily. The bus was old and appeared to be in dire need of repairs. The brakes creaked and jolted, and there didn't seem to be any suspension. Moira and I were sitting at the back, and whenever we went over a bump we were ejected from our seats, our heads almost touching the ceiling.

I would have been petrified, but there was no point. There was no way to leave the bus and, if we did, we'd be in the middle of nowhere—which could be even more frightening than the prospect of tumbling over the mountain side. We were stuck. This was one ride that had to be taken.

Moira and I squeezed each other's hands and giggled.

We looked wide-eyed through the windows. We hurtled through tiny villages, where candles burned and people huddled in the streets, talking and eating. We picked up the scents of rice fields and aromatic plants.

The driver's incense continued to burn, and we were safe in its plume, mingled with the smoke of cigarettes and charcoal fires at the road side.

Our senses were completely alive.

We rode the moment.

Connecting the dots

Traveling through Asia had been surreal. We'd been to so many exotic places and taken away a kaleidoscope of memories — people, smells, tastes and colors. Moira and I were sad when we realized our journey was coming to a close.

Despite all of those memories, and for all the highs and lows of our travels, I remained haunted by the image of the young boy with cerebral palsy, begging on the floor. I kept reliving the look we exchanged.

Family, I had thought. People with disabilities, connected to one another by powerful, invisible bonds.

With our wheelchairs, our atrophied legs, our spasmy bodies, our unpredictable bladders, our determination, our strength, our creative ideas, our empathy, our passion for justice, our yearning for equality, we are related. Yes, our lives are diverse, but there is a deep core of understanding that comes from shared experience.

I realized, however, that there were few means by which we could hear each others' stories, listen to each others' nightmares, see each others' dreams. We were scattered. We were isolated. Some of us never made the connections that we needed to experience that sense of kinship.

Somehow, I needed to try to make those connections happen.

It wasn't enough just to organize sports and recreation programs, like I had in Berkeley and Brisbane. More was needed — much more. My travels had taught me that there were links to be made all over the world.

When we arrived in London, Moira and I bought ourselves hamburgers just to relax and enjoy a familiar meal — one, ironically, that we would probably never eat at home.

And then it was time to say goodbye. Moira returned to Nova Scotia, and I boarded a plane for Oregon.

Oregon.

I wondered what it would be like.

I had a Master's degree to complete — and then what? There was a world of "family" to think about. I was starting to connect the dots, and I needed to keep figuring out links.

The plane door closed. An adrenaline-filled part of my life was closing, too. I was sad because I wasn't sure it would ever be like that again.

Luckily, I didn't know how right I was.

9.

We grabbed a notebook. The dirty dishes could wait. Ideas were flowing. There were no naysayers here — no one to dampen our dreams or say they weren't realistic. We were two idealistic friends in a small kitchen where anything seemed possible.

Lost in the USA

The transition to Oregon would not be easy. I'd had a magical year, and I experienced what is known in the exchange field as "re-entry" — a sense of being culturally lost. I'd gone back to the United States, but I hadn't gone "home". I missed Australia and felt strangely like a foreigner.

I was now in a mellow land of tofu and vegetarians. People spoke slowly and sat around having potluck dinners, talking about mundane things that bored me. Oregon seemed gray and rainy. Rod moved from Berkeley to be closer to me and was majoring in recreation and computer science, but I still longed for sunny Australia, going to barbeques, eating Vegemite for breakfast, hearing a friendly "G'day", and being an honorary Aussie. Travel experiences with Moira were fresh in my memory, and I yearned for the rush of excitement that had greeted each day.

At night, a mishmash of memories filtered into my dreams.

Riding on a Goldwing motorcycle with wind in my hair. Fields of newly cut sugar cane. The feel of a cuddly koala. The colors of the Olgas. Incense on Thai buses. An old buffalo tilling sodden fields.

Soon, I began boring those around me with stories of Australia and travels through New Zealand, Indonesia, Malaysia and Thailand.

"Susan, you are in Oregon now," they'd gently remind me. "It's time to move on."

Deep down, I knew they were right. It was time to admit that Eugene, Oregon, was my new home. I needed to concentrate on my studies and be satisfied with the present.

Yet I remained unsettled. I realized that my disorientation and sense of being a foreigner came partly from a feeling that I had become, above all, a citizen of the world. I had also come to recognize — and begun to explore — the idea of "family" among people with disabilities.

It was a powerful notion, and it wouldn't let me rest.

When an opportunity arose, I decided to take a break and visit some friends in England and Europe.

At the time I wasn't sure what I was looking for. Somehow, I found it anyway.

Serendipity

One of the friends I visited in England was Stuart. I'd met Stuart back in my Berkeley days, while he was touring the USA looking at innovative recreation programs for disabled people. As an artist, poet, playwright, Shakespearean actor, singer and puppeteer, Stuart was one of the most creative and talented people I had ever met. He used all of these skills in running a series of programs in Portsmouth, a historic seaport in southern England, with the aim of linking kids from high risk backgrounds with young people with a range of disabilities. I had been thrilled when he came to Berkeley to look at BORP, staying in the apartment I shared with Diane.

That might have been where things ended. My visit to Portsmouth ensured that it wasn't.

Stuart lived by himself in a small apartment, up several flights of stairs. I thought I'd stay a few nights, just to catch up. In fact, I was so captivated by his creativity and imagination that my three-day day visit turned into a three-week adventure.

How could I leave? Stuart took me to ancient ruins where he recited sonnets. He sang songs in Welsh, Hebrew and Arabic. He spontaneously performed plays with marionettes and puppets. He created theater at the dinner table using salt and pepper shakers as the main characters, with cutlery as the supporting cast. He was funny and witty — and poor, as many true artists are. Often there was little food in the house, and we invented gourmet dishes using the last remaining cans at the back of the cupboard. I loved every minute of it.

I met Stuart's friends — actors, poets and magicians. I met the students he worked with, watched Stuart develop plays with them, always making them central to the creative process.

One day, Stuart also introduced me to Tony Lumley.

The serendipity of life has always astonished me. Fortuitous introductions, chance encounters, overheard conversations and decisions made on the run can change our destinies and, in turn, change the destinies of others.

121

Tony Lumley and a wonderful man from Denmark, Bruno Manson, were the founders of Mobility International, and Tony ran the organization from London. Mobility International (MI) facilitated cultural exchanges for young people with disabilities, working from Europe to the Middle East. At the time, it was very innovative. They were getting folks in wheelchairs camping in the Bahraini deserts, and enabling blind youth from France to go to Ireland. Chapters of MI had been established in a number of countries, which operated completely independently. Tony was interested in establishing a branch in the USA. There had been one fruitless attempt already.

Stuart thought I would be just the right person to make it happen.

By the time I returned to Eugene, Oregon, so did I.

I made a plan with a friend, Barbara Williams, who was working toward her PhD in therapeutic recreation while I was finishing my Master's degree. Both of us came from a more radical disability rights framework than MI, but we agreed that being part of an international network of chapters with so many countries represented was intriguing, offering opportunities that were exceptional. We put our heads together and formed a non profit organization called MIUSA (Mobility International USA).

Barbara and I then decided to drive my old van to Toronto, Canada, for a MI conference with the intention of securing our nomination as MI's official USA chapter. We received a $500 donation from a Rotarian in Eugene who believed in our dreams, and Eugene's Rotary Club matched it. One thousand dollars was all we had to pay our expenses and conference costs, as well as get our organization up and running. In the beginning, we were under the auspices of the Lane County Low Riders wheelchair basketball team.

In 1981, we set out on that long journey to the east coast and back — over six thousand miles. It was the beginning of an odyssey that would change my life, and the lives of many others.

Toronto by van

Barbara and I slept almost every night in the van on a drive that took us across the sweet-smelling cornfields of Iowa and many other states of the USA. We spent hours listening to music, gazing out of windows, eating at truck stops and buying food at local markets.

We arrived in Toronto tired but excited, and in our quest to save money decided to continue sleeping in the van. When we pulled into a parking space at the conference center, we noticed a man behaving strangely in the car next to us. He was bare-chested and seemed unnecessarily curious about our sleeping arrangements, which made us so uncomfortable that we moved the van to the other side of the parking lot. As we were getting ready for the night, Barbara got out of the van to move our mattresses into place, and was startled to see the man walking toward our van wearing even less clothes than he had been wearing before. She jumped into the van.

"Start the car!"

I lunged toward the steering wheel and drove away as fast as I could.

Our sense of security shaken, I turned into the driveway of

an emergency room at a nearby hospital. Exhausted after our journey and now in my pajamas, I explained our predicament and asked if we could sleep in the more secure hospital parking lot, or on a couch in a waiting room. They agreed to the parking lot, and we did our best to settle down for the night with bright lights glaring in our faces. In the morning, we washed in the hospital bathrooms and tried to make ourselves presentable before returning to the conference center.

We were greeted at registration by folks with disabilities from many countries including Bahrain, Grenada, Malta, Kenya, Trinidad and France. I was amazed at how fast Barbara and I made friends with other delegates.

Later, during the General Assembly, Mobility International USA (MIUSA) was officially adopted as a chapter of MI. Not only that, but I was elected as a vice president on the board of the London-based organization.

I might have been sleeping in a parking lot, but my international career was skyrocketing!

Big breakfast

Barbara and I were suddenly in a position to do what we had dreamed of doing. The only immediate problem we faced was funding, so after the conference we drove to New York for a breakfast meeting with Eugene Ferkauf, the father of one of my high school friends. He was an affluent philanthropist, and we met him at his favorite restaurant in New York. Although it was a classy establishment, the general ambience was relaxed, and he arrived dressed in a plain sweatshirt and simple trousers.

We babbled on and on about MIUSA—our ideas, our hopes and our dreams. Mr. Ferkauf listened carefully, and gave us his advice about various aspects of the infant organization and some possible programs. After a while, he asked us a question.

"So what do you need?"

"Funding," I replied sheepishly.

"How much?"

I hesitated. I had absolutely no idea how much to ask for. What would be considered too much? Perhaps he'd think us foolish if we asked for too little?

"Ten thousand dollars," I blurted out. I had no idea where that amount came from—and I still don't.

"I'll give you five," Mr. Ferkauf said with a smile.

"Really?"

I was astonished. Here was a man who was agreeing to give us five thousand dollars over some scrambled eggs—simply because he liked our ideas and our enthusiasm. No matter how affluent you are, that's generous. I would forever be grateful.

Barbara and I finished our breakfasts and left with bellies full and minds racing. We had come a long way fast, and there now seemed to be almost endless possibilities in front of us.

There was a lot of work to do. We were eager to take it on.

Challenge and change

We drove back over mountains and plains to Oregon, pondering how to make the best use of our opportunities to empower people with disabilities through exchanges and training.

By the time we arrived in Eugene we were very tired, and our clothes badly needed a wash. It didn't matter. We were energized and invigorated by our dreams.

MIUSA, we believed, could facilitate visits to the USA by people with disabilities from throughout the world. People would not only meet other disabled folks, but could volunteer to work on projects together, go river rafting, do challenge courses. They'd be encouraged to defy all preconceived notions of what disabled people could and couldn't do.

Late at night, at the kitchen table of the house Barbara and I shared, we came up with the phrase, *Challenge yourself and change the world!*

"I can imagine young kids with disabilities growing up dreaming of becoming citizen diplomats," I said to Barbara while clearing away some dishes.

Thinking about the boy I had seen in Thailand, with his twisted legs, spasmy body and fascination with my wheelchair, I kept coming back to the idea of family—a global family of people with disabilities.

"Yes," said Barbara. "Why not? People with disabilities and their non-disabled allies—like me —could share ideas about how about getting equal rights, education, jobs, transportation, recreation, and more. We wouldn't meet in formal conferences, we'd talk while camping under the stars. We'll discuss politics while peeling potatoes. We could arrange homestays with families in the community, instead of using fancy hotels which no one can afford."

"Yes! Yes!"

I grabbed a notebook. The dirty dishes could wait. The ideas were flowing and there was no one around to say they weren't practical. We were just two idealistic friends in a small kitchen where anything seemed possible.

I knew that I'd need to call upon everything I had learned while running BORP, and during my experiences as a Rotary ambassador in Australia.

Barbara was writing furiously in the note book.

"Why shouldn't disabled people take the lead and get international experiences that would enable them to get Fulbright scholarships, or join the Peace Corps, or become ambassadors and international consultants. I can imagine a young teenager in a wheelchair studying in Spain to learn Spanish, a Deaf student getting a Master's degree in Kenya, a blind high school student spending a year abroad in Germany."

"Yes! Yes! Write it all down!"

The excitement was mounting. Fuelled by milk and chocolate chip cookies, we developed a vision based on leadership training run by and for disabled people. Participants would do everything from building ramps to sharing songs around a fireplace, taking home strategies that would change their lives and improve the lives of others in their communities.

They were big dreams, but even the largest of dreams have the smallest of beginnings.

Challenge yourself and change the world!

That seemed to say it all.

It was well past midnight. We put away the few remaining cookies and, with smiles on our faces, got ready for bed.

10.

People were discussing politics under the stars. Friendships were formed while peeling potatoes. Disabled and non-disabled folks were volunteering side by side as equals.

Tom

Oh my gosh… Is he tall!

He was well over six feet and incredibly good looking, with dark hair, big brown eyes and long eyelashes. He towered over me, smiling as I opened the door. There was a twinkle in his eye, and his self-confident manner reminded me a little of Stuart, although physically there was very little resemblance. Stuart was short and thin, while this man looked like a lumberjack — perhaps even a redwood tree.

I was leaving a meeting of the Oregon Women and Leisure (OWL) group, comprised of students and professionals in the recreation field interested in sharing ideas and information. The group included professors from the University of Oregon but most women were like me, students working toward higher degrees in community, therapeutic or outdoor recreation. OWL met every few weeks in someone's house to discuss the latest trends, talk about our aspirations and, of course, have a potluck meal, usually vegetarian.

"Who are you?" I asked.

"I'm Tom," he said with a grin.

He told me that he lived there—his sister had hosted our meeting. I opened the door wider to let him through, and went on my way.

If there was ever the possibility of forgetting about this tall, handsome man, the next few weeks made it impossible. Eugene is a relatively small town—back then, there were only about 100,000 people. Tom and I kept running into each other, just like that first time. We always seemed to be in the same stores, or sitting across from each other in restaurants, or sharing the same bike paths. There were so many coincidental meetings that we eventually took out our calendars and arranged to meet for coffee.

Although I was attracted to him, I was still dating Rod. Tom was also in a relationship, so it seemed clear to both of us that our friendship was just that—a friendship, and no more.

Whenever we got together we had a wonderful time. Tom continued to remind me of Stuart—he was very theatrical, and sang beautifully. Twelve years older than me, he was a member of a barbershop quartet and loved singing songs by Fred Astaire, Frank Sinatra and Tony Bennett. That wasn't my kind of music—I preferred Judy Collins and Joni Mitchell—but I definitely enjoyed being around someone so lively and expressive, a man who liked being around people and didn't mind being the center of attention. In so many ways, he seemed the opposite of Rod.

Tom and I continued to run into each other and meet occasionally for coffee. Our friendship became deeper, and I treasured it.

Overwhelmed

Living with Barbara was fun and my life was very full. In addition to my usual student responsibilities of studying, taking exams and writing papers, there was the adrenaline rush of starting a new organization.

I was still missing my life in Australia, but the thought of being able to connect people from around the world lifted my spirits and made Oregon feel more like home. Barbara and I were organizing our first program, which would bring disabled and non-disabled people from eleven different countries to Eugene. I resurrected my famous chocolate fondue recipe and began bringing it to various pot luck parties, symbolically uniting my two lives.

But just as all was looking wonderful, Barbara made an announcement.

"You're going to *what?*" I asked incredulously.

"I'm going to get married."

She had been dating a Taiwanese student who was brilliant with computers. I knew they were close, but her news caught me by surprise.

"Wow," I said. "That's great!"

I hoped I sounded convincing because, inside, I wasn't so sure. I knew it meant that Barbara would soon be moving out of the lovely house we shared in a quiet, tree-lined street not far from the university.

"Susan, he wants me to move to California — to Silicon Valley where all the good jobs in computing are. He wants me to go

131

with him."

My stomach knotted.

"When?"

The look on Barbara's face told me that I wouldn't like the answer. "In a few months," she replied quietly.

"A few months! You can't! We haven't even run our first exchange program. You're the co- director, you're my housemate… Do you have to move away?"

Barbara was broken-hearted to have to choose between leaving MIUSA and getting married, but her fiancé was adamant that he needed to go to California to be successful. I was happy for Barbara, but couldn't avoid the grip of panic. I would be the sole director of MIUSA. I would also need to find a new housemate or, even worse, another place to live.

After a few months, Barbara left for California, and it was sad and difficult moment for both of us. It was all very daunting, and I was a little overwhelmed.

A subtle transition

"Tom, you won't believe what Barbara has told me."

"What?"

Tom had a Master's degree in social work and extensive experience in counseling. He was really great at listening to my problems and being completely engaged.

"She's getting married and moving to California. There goes my co-director — and my roommate. I'm happy for her but I'm totally freaking out. What am I going to do?"

Tom had a calming effect on me as we discussed my options.

"Roommates are not so hard to find. That's really the least of your problems."

"No, I think I'm done with roommates. I'd like to have my own place—and maybe get a dog."

"What about MIUSA?"

"I guess I'm on my own there," I replied. I felt my stress level rise as I thought about finishing postgraduate studies while organizing the first MIUSA program and also finding a new place to live. It all seemed too much for me to cope with, and Tom could see it.

"Hey, you need a break to clear your head. Would you like to go camping for the weekend, just to get away from it all?"

It was a lovely offer.

"Yeah, sure, I guess, but I don't have time to organize anything. I'm too snowed under."

"No problem. Leave it to me," Tom said confidently. "I'll pick you up next Saturday. Just bring your sleeping bag."

I didn't really think about the camping trip too much—I had too much else to think about. On the following Saturday, Tom came to pick me up in his 1973 Land Rover. It looked like the vehicles I had seen in *Out of Africa*.

This might be fun, I thought. I climbed into the front seat, by the window, leaving the middle seat empty. Suddenly, it occurred to me that I was going away with a guy who was not my boyfriend and I became a little self-conscious. Rod had gone back to Nevada for a few weeks to see his old friends and family. *Not to worry*, I thought. *Tom and I are friends.*

On the way to the mountains, Tom stopped at a grocery

store. He already had the Land Rover packed with a tent, charcoal, lanterns and food. What else could he possibly need?

I waited, curious.

When Tom returned, he handed me a big pack of peanut M&Ms. My favorite. My heart skipped a beat.

The campsite was breathtaking, with pine trees surrounding a tranquil lake. We went out in Tom's canoe, and I swam in the cool, clear water. All my problems were washed away, at least for the moment.

Tom made a delicious meal, and we talked and laughed for hours. I slept under the stars, my sleeping bag zipped tight so that I didn't project any invitations. *We are friends*, I told myself. *Nothing more.*

On our way home the next day, we stopped to share a root beer float. It felt natural. At some point, there had been a transition—very subtle, but very real. It no longer seemed right to be sitting next to the window in his car. Now, I was sitting next to him in the middle seat. My heart was beating faster than normal. Something had changed. Our relationship had taken a turn.

When we arrived at my house, my eyes widened and I felt sick. Rod's red Volvo was there—he had come back from Nevada early. Nothing had happened between Tom and I on our camping trip, but I felt guilty.

Unsteady, unsure.

"Tom, could you drive around the block for a minute. I just need a minute to think."

Tom sensed that I was uncomfortable. He felt it too.

"I can't see you again for a while," I said. "I had a really good time, though."

"So did I," he replied.

"I need to figure things out with Rod. Right now I'm a bit confused. I'll call you in a couple of weeks."

"That's fine, Susan. Take your time." Tom's voice was calm and reassuring.

I got out of the Land Rover, went into my house and met Rod's eyes. They contained deep sadness.

I think we knew that it was the beginning of the end for us. I was as sad as he was—I loved Rod, and cherished all that we had shared. Perhaps I always knew that we were too different for our relationship to last forever. Confronting that wasn't easy, but I couldn't ignore the feelings I was developing for Tom.

From the moment Tom handed me that bag of M&Ms, things had begun to change.

Turmoil

Breaking up with Rod was excruciating—one of the most awful experiences I've had.

Why would I break up with him? He was kind and gentle. He was extremely smart, and insightful. We had traveled through Europe, climbed aboard buses in Latin America and swum in the turquoise waters of the Caribbean. We had scaled the Acropolis and Masada, and skied down slopes in Switzerland. Rod was my friend, my lover and my teacher.

But something was missing. We reflected our backgrounds in so many ways. I was the gregarious New Yorker, accustomed to a fast-paced lifestyle and needing the company of others, while he was the man from rural Nevada, with a much greater need for quiet and solitude.

For me, it was all about the vast difference in our personalities. We talked about this soon after my camping trip, while sitting in Rod's Saab. Rod listened from a place of deep pain and heard a reason that had never once entered my thoughts.

"Well, it's no surprise", he said miserably. "You got some non-disabled guy."

It stung. Rod's accusation reflected a stereotype that I loathed. In fact, his disability was a hugely positive aspect of our relationship. We had so many things in common, including our passion for international travel and wheelchair sports.

"That's not true Rod, your disability has nothing to with it. Please, *please* don't say that."

"I guess I just wasn't good enough for you," he mumbled.

"No, Rod. No. That's not true. You know it's not. You were the best thing that ever happened to me. I love you. You're the best lover I've ever had. Please don't say all these things."

He had stopped listening. I was struck by the dreadful thought that this was all reminding him of his other big break-up — when his wife left him after his accident. But I couldn't go there.

I cried and cried. Rod stared through the window of his car. It was clear that he wanted the discussion to be over. Nothing I said was making anything better. I wanted to hang on to every last moment being with him, but I realized it wasn't fair. I needed to let him go. I had hurt him. I would have been hurt too. Eventually I put us both out of our misery and let him drop me off at home.

The next few weeks were difficult. I felt incredibly sad, and couldn't help doubting my actions. I thought about Tom but didn't call because I knew I needed to be certain of my feelings.

Deep inside, though, I knew that everything that had happened was meant to be. I'd done the right thing. Rod and I had been a team. In the future, I hoped, we could be friends.

Breaking barriers

Perhaps fortunately, there was little time to dwell on things. I needed to regroup. I also needed to move out of the beautiful house I had been sharing with Barbara, and to make sure that the first MIUSA program proved a success.

After looking around for a place to live, I decided on a house that looked like it was made for a munchkin. It was the tiniest house I ever saw, but I adored it. Tom, who could build anything and knew a lot about renovation, came over to help me paint the halls. We began dating each other, and I fell in love.

I also adopted a dog at the pound, a mutt which seemed to have some German Shepherd heritage. I named him "Yofee", which means "very special" in Hebrew. Although he was a bit nasty to other people, he quickly became affectionate and protective toward me, which made me feel safe living alone.

With a lot of hard work at MIUSA, our plans took shape. Soon the big day arrived and eleven young people arrived from other countries to work on a range of community service projects around Eugene, including the making of wheelchair accessible trails at a summer camp. Most came from countries such as Bahrain, Germany, Sweden, England and Denmark. Some in the group seemed surprised that the director of the program was herself disabled, and it immediately changed group dynamics. In volunteering to help the disabled, they simply hadn't expected "the disabled" to be in charge. There was a lesson in that for everyone.

For three weeks, we slept in sleeping bags at the various sites and prepared most of our meals ourselves. With only a shoestring budget, I was thankful that lots of food had been donated, and Tom volunteered to drive the big yellow school bus we used. He would sing to us on the bus and was loved by all the participants, also helping organize our work projects because he knew so much about building.

Nick had come from Germany to join the program. He was tall, lean and full of mischief, bonding immediately with Anders, a blond and intelligent young man from Sweden. Both were non-disabled, and being only seventeen years-old seemed caught between wanting to "help disabled people" and wanting to break all the rules, just like other teenagers. One day, they were scolded by the director of the very conservative summer camp for taking an early morning "skinny dip". Nude swimming was just not part of the accepted behavior, even though there were no campers present at the time.

Seiyu had come from Japan and used an electric wheelchair. He was a bit older — in his early thirties — and was smart and witty. At home, his family helped him with bathing and dressing, and he was accustomed to ritual bathing and lots of care and attention. He had arrived without any personal assistants, however, and it was quite a shock adapting to a bathing routine that consisted of Nick or Anders hosing him down like a car at a group shower facility.

Barb Yost, a friend of mine from the University of Oregon, had been employed to help me run the program after Barbara

Williams moved to California with her husband. She was loud and energetic, with bright, blonde hair and a carefree attitude. We soon became familiar with her battle cry in the mornings — "Five minutes! Five minutes!" — as she tried to rouse folks from their sleeping bags after they had stayed up late talking and dancing. Her endless energy and wild remarks kept everyone on their toes.

"Nice buns," Barb could often be heard saying, remarking on some guy's physique. It counterbalanced the guys in the group, who were always eyeing the women in their scanty summer work outfits.

But amidst all this joking and flirting, important work was accomplished. Somehow, it all worked. Disabled and non-disabled folks were working side-by-side as equals. Ramps and wheelchair accessible trails were built and other trails were cleaned up and expanded. One of our projects was to construct ramps in the non-profit retreat center where I now lived, called "Shivtei Shalom". Shivtei Shalom was a "moshav", or small kibbutz, in Oregon — started by mostly Jewish families who wanted to live cooperatively and spiritually on collectively owned land. It was a surprise to Essam from Bahrain and some of the other delegates when Friday night came, and we all sat around a table singing Hebrew and Arabic songs with the rabbi of the synagogue who lived on the moshav. Barriers that kept different cultures separated — like the barriers that separated disabled and non-disabled folks — were being dismantled and replaced by shared food and laughter. People were discussing politics under the stars, and friendships were being formed while peeling potatoes. Besides volunteering, the group was able to see summer snow at Mount Hood, and visit the breathtaking Oregon coast.

For me, every day was both exciting and exhausting. During this first program, all that I could think about was the next meal, the next activity. Even when it was over, I had no real idea about the global impact that MIUSA would make. Parting with the participants was emotional, but I was happy.

I finished my Master's degree and was able to put all my time and energy into MIUSA. Soon afterward, my parents asked me to go away with them for a vacation. I invited Tom to stay in my home to take care of Yofee. He did, and he never left. All my dreams were coming true. Life was sweet. Sometimes, you just have to stop and be grateful for your good fortune.

Then, just like so many times before, just when all seemed perfect, the bubble burst.

11.

Regret and holding on to the past would not be helpful, and I concentrated on positive thoughts and let a new chapter of my life unfold. I naively told myself that this would be my last life-changing medical challenge.

Syringowhat?

I was on an airplane, heading away for a vacation with my parents. Mobility International USA (MIUSA) was already a success, and I was full of ideas about its future development. I was in love with Tom and he was at home with Yofee.

So why on earth was I looking out the window with tears streaming down my face?

I knew something was wrong. Very wrong.

A tingling sensation, much like pins and needles, stretched up my right arm to my neck, and into half my face. I tried telling myself that it was a pinched nerve, something insignificant and temporary.

It will go soon.

Any minute now...

Who was I trying to kid? I'd already had the sensation for days. How much longer could I go on pretending it was nothing?

When I returned home, I called my neurosurgeon friend Dr. Gene Bolles in Colorado. I was sent for an MRI—at the time, fairly new diagnostic imaging technology—in Eugene.

Straight afterward, the doctor delivered my results.

"You have syringomyelia," he said. His face was sad, sympathetic—but there was something phony about it, as if he practiced the expression for such occasions.

"Syringowhat?"

I'd never heard of such a thing. I could barely pronounce it and I definitely couldn't spell it, but I needed to know what it meant.

"Syringomyelia," the doctor said in his monotone. "It's a liquid cyst that is very rare, but can form in your spinal cord after spinal injury. I'm afraid you will need to have surgery. A shunt will be put in to drain the cyst."

While he was admiring the accuracy of the MRI and the extraordinary length of the cyst, which of course was nothing but terrible news to me, I went into shock. Again I was facing a complicated medical intervention, and I dreaded it.

I began researching my newly acquired condition. None of it sounded good. Syringomyelia could cause a loss of muscle function and could even be fatal. Some people had surgery to insert a shunt, while some did nothing and lost the use of their arms or other body parts. It was all a nightmare. There seemed no way out, but the shunt was my best option.

I spoke with Dr. Bolles and he offered to fly to Eugene at his own expense and assist with the operation. My spirits lifted immediately. We went out to dinner at a jazz club the night before the surgery, with my parents and Tom. After all he'd done for me in the past, I was so comforted to have Gene with me.

What I didn't really understand was that it would take a full two years to recover from the surgery. I would have pain and discomfort. I would always have some sort of tingling in my hand and arm, varying in degree.

That was bearable. More significant for me was that any rotation of my right shoulder would cause greater discomfort and threaten me with the possibility of arresting the shunt, which was likely to cause loss of muscle function.

Once again, my life was forced to change.

I could no longer play wheelchair basketball, one of my greatest loves. I had been instrumental in starting two women's basketball teams, one in Berkeley and one in Eugene.

I could no longer play wheelchair tennis, which was an exciting emerging sport.

I could no longer play table tennis, a sport I had competed in nationally, taking first place in my division three times.

I gave up skiing. I had learned to ski on the beautiful slopes of Winter Park and Aspen, Colorado, and I had even skied with my adaptive equipment in Switzerland. This had involved standing up with the aid of crutches connected to mini skis, called "outriggers", which complemented the skis on my feet. I had later used an adapted ski called a "sit ski", effectively a kind of narrow sled with a single ski under it, with two short "outriggers" for balance.

Those days were over.

Typing or writing caused my hand to cramp up and spasm, so I limited it as far as possible and had an assistant do all my correspondence and computer work at MIUSA.

I remembered the words of Bill, from the rehab center in

Manhattan so many years ago.

That life is over. This life is here. They are separate.

I tried to let my athletic life go, and embrace once again the new life I had been given. I learned that there were still sports that I *could* do, those which didn't cause me to rotate my shoulder. I began cycling, either on a tandem bike or independently on an adapted tricycle with an electrical assist in the front wheel. With a friend, I was able to buy a horse that had been specially trained to respond to voice commands.

Yet inevitably, there was sadness in my loss. It was the second time I'd had to give up so many activities that I loved, activities that seemed to have become part of my identity.

At the same time, I understood that regret and holding on to the past would not be helpful. I concentrated on positive thoughts and let a new chapter of my life unfold. Surely, I told myself naively, this would be my last life-changing medical challenge. In the back of my mind was the often quoted wisdom: *We cannot control what happens to us in life, but we can control how we react to those changes or challenges.*

Sex talk in Costa Rica

I had gone to Costa Rica for a few days, and the purpose of my visit was sex.

Not *having* sex, I hasten to add, but *talking* about it.

I'd been invited to lead a two-day seminar in San Jose, speaking on the taboo topic of sexuality and people with disabilities. Although I was no expert on the subject, I knew from my own experiences with both disabled and non-disabled men that sex was both possible and enjoyable. I believed it was important to talk about it.

My audience was comprised mostly of rehabilitation doctors and therapists—around one hundred and fifty of them—and I wanted them to understand that disability does not diminish desire and need not impede the practice or satisfaction of sex. If health professionals don't understand this, their advice to newly disabled folks can only be flawed, needlessly leading to depression and loneliness.

The seminar seemed to go well. I told participants of the bumper stickers in California that read: *Quads Make Better Lovers*. I also related how, long ago, when I told my mother that my new boyfriend was a paraplegic, she had looked at me with disbelief.

"Why would you want a boyfriend who is paralyzed from the waist down?" she had asked.

Being partially paralyzed from the waist down myself, I'd found that amusing. When I explained to my mom that he was a great lover, she had still looked puzzled. Neither of us was eager to discuss this in more detail, so the conversation had switched to what we should have for dinner.

The main focus of my sex and disability seminar in San Jose was self-esteem. I spoke of body image, and ways to adapt lovemaking techniques. Since many spinal cord injured people have limited sensation and movement, I said, creativity was the key.

There was only one hitch.

Because a majority in the audience spoke English as a second language or not at all, I had requested a professional Spanish translator. Unfortunately, the translator was hurt when he fell out of his wheelchair during our lunch break, and he needed to leave the seminar. That left me to explain the benefits of oral sex and whole-body arousal techniques in not very accurate Spanish. It wasn't easy.

To this day, I do not know exactly what I told people to do. I just remember that the room was silent, all eyes and ears fixated on every word I was saying.

Whatever I said, I hope it worked!

Narrow escape

My trip to Costa Rica was destined to have sexual overtones, no matter where I went. Amazingly, three separate encounters had "adult themes", as television censorship warnings say.

In a coffee break at the seminar, a young doctor offered to pick me up the next day and take me on a tour of a nearby volcano. I gratefully accepted, not knowing that the soundtrack to the tour would become a barrage of rather personal questions, beginning with "Just how much can you feel below your waist?" and going way beyond the domain of professional interest. I was relieved when my private tour finished. The volcano may have been active, but that doctor's mind was definitely *over*active.

Later, I was enjoying the sunshine on a beautiful beach flanking one side of a national park several hours outside San Jose. The waves were rolling in, leaving white foam to bubble gently on wet sand. Tired of pushing my wheelchair, I had maneuvered myself so that I could sit on the sand. I hugged my knees to my chest and inhaled deeply, loving the ocean air and the solitude.

Before long I noticed someone approaching me. A young, attractive girl was making a beeline for me, looking slightly embarrassed but very determined. I could see that she wanted to ask me something.

How odd, I found myself thinking. *I'm sitting beside a wheelchair on a remote beach in a foreign country, and I'm about to give directions or dispense some kind of advice.*

"Excuse me," the girl said. She was perhaps seventeen or eighteen, and was speaking to me in Spanish.

"May I ask you a question?"

"Sure," I replied, hoping it would be a simple question — something like directions to the nearest bathroom. "But speak slowly and simply. My Spanish is not that good."

She began a long and complicated story, and I was soon thinking that my Spanish was worse than I thought. Either that, or I was having a bizarre dream. What I *thought* she was saying couldn't possibly be true, could it?

With a very puzzled look on my face, I asked her to repeat her story and her question.

The girl patiently reiterated everything and, to my surprise, I realized that I'd understood her properly the first time. She was staying with her boyfriend in a nearby hotel. He was married — but that wasn't what was worrying her. What she really wanted was sexual advice. In particular, she wanted to know about anal sex. Should she do it? Would it hurt? Could she get a disease? What should she do if her boyfriend got angry when she refused? Reading between the lines, I saw that her boyfriend had already gotten angry, presumably because she'd been hesitant.

This was not a topic I was comfortable with, and I had no

idea why this beautiful girl would approach a perfect stranger and ask such personal questions.

What did I do?

I gave her the best advice I could think of.

She thanked me and walked away, as mysteriously as she had approached me. I told myself that any connection with my seminar was impossible, and that being regarded as a sex expert so soon afterward could only be a coincidence. I felt sure that this would be my last brush with Costa Rican sexuality but, unfortunately, it wasn't.

Earlier that day, I'd met the director of the national park on a dirt path lined with palm trees, running along the edge of the beach. He was a tall, fit looking man in a khaki uniform, with a well-combed mustache and thick black hair. There were very few American tourists around, and a woman in a wheelchair traveling by herself always seems to invite conversation. After my encounter with the girl on the beach, I was on my way back to my very basic hotel when I saw the director again. He smiled broadly.

"What are you doing for dinner?"

"Oh, nothing in particular. I'm here by myself."

"May I join you?"

"Sure," I said.

"I'll meet you at eight o'clock at the outside restaurant."

"Great!"

When evening arrived, the first thing I noticed was that the "outside restaurant" was a very romantic place. You could hear the ocean, just a few hundred feet away, and there were candles on every table. Soon Mr. Park Ranger appeared, wearing a crisp white shirt and dark pants. His name was Antonio.

148

Uh oh, I thought. Even so, I was flattered that the head of the national park wanted to have dinner with me, and he did look nice. These shallow, superficial thoughts should have set my alarm bells ringing. Obviously I wasn't thinking clearly – my intuition and experience in self-preservation were abandoning me. I didn't see it at the time, but I was headed for trouble.

We conversed about the usual things — why I was in Costa Rica, how long he'd been working in the park, and so on. He kept calling me "Suzanne", and I decided not to correct him because it made me feel exotic. I remember encouraging him to make the park more wheelchair-accessible, possibly the only intelligent thing that I said.

Then, somehow, Antonio turned our conversation to the subject of the park's insects.

"You know, Suzanne, they are very troublesome. They are large, and if they get in your bed and bite you, they suck out your blood. That is why this park is so deserted. Most tourists are staying away."

"You are kidding me, aren't you?"

I dreaded his response.

"No, no. *Es serioso*," he replied, reverting to Spanish for emphasis.

I *hate* insects and spiders. The thought of blood sucking insects adhering to my body in the middle of the night was more than I could bear. It sent a chill right through me, and I excused myself so that I could get my sweater from the hotel room. While I was there, I saw several giant cockroaches scurry across the floor. I pushed as fast as I could back to the restaurant.

"What is it Suzanne?" Antonio spoke gently, like a father to an upset child.

I described my horrifying encounter with the bugs he had just warned me about. I knew that I'd never be able to sleep with them in my room, and I was too disgusted to even think about killing them with my shoes. I planned to stay up all night. I didn't care if Antonio thought me silly. I was the victim of a serious phobia.

"*No se preocupa,*" he said, taking my hand. "Don't worry. I'll take care of you."

That sounded good. He would come and kill the bugs and then spray the room, and I'd be safe. So what if the room reeked of pesticide? I could deal with that—better than being eaten alive by blood sucking cockroach-like vampires!

But Antonio had different ideas. The bugs, he said, were not affected by pesticides, and they came up in a constant procession from the beach. If you killed a few, more would come.

"But what can I do?" It never occurred to me to think about how the few other tourists were surviving in their rooms.

"Suzanne, I will come as your friend and stay in your room. If I see any bugs I will kill them. You will be able to sleep. Please, I want to do this for you."

"Are you sure?" I hoped he wouldn't change his mind.

Women travelers around the world, please take note: this is what is called an "error of judgment." A really serious error of judgment.

"*Si estoy seguro.*"

Antonio followed me up to my room. He killed a few bugs with his sandals and, for the moment, no others appeared.

"Please lie down and sleep," he said.

I lay down on the bed, beginning to feel the awkwardness of the situation. I reasoned with myself: *He is a park ranger, the director of the national park. I am fully clothed. It will be fine.*

It wasn't fine. Within a few minutes he had locked the door and was lying down next to me.

That's strange, I thought. *How is he going to see the bugs and kill them if he is lying down? Bugs can get under the door, so why did he lock it?*

He turned off the bedside light and my sense of panic escalated. Still, I tried to convince myself that I was being paranoid. I closed my eyes, heard his heavy breathing in the dark. Several minutes passed. Then, very stealthily, his hand alighted on my thigh. I removed it. A few minutes later I had to move it away again. Next, I felt his large hand near my breast. I grabbed it and pushed it away forcefully, so there could be no doubt about my unwillingness. Even that didn't stop him. Within a few seconds, he was again trying to caress my inner thigh.

"No," I said firmly.

"Okay, sorry," Antonio said. But he soon tried again.

"No," I repeated. There was anger in my voice, but I must also have sounded scared.

He waited awhile before his next attempt which, by then, I knew would come. My heart was beating like a drum. I felt absolute terror. I was certain that I was about to be raped. This man had not forced his way into my room—I had let him in. If he raped me, it would be my word against his.

Antonio had moved my wheelchair to the other side of the room, away from the bed. There was no way of reaching it without crawling on the floor. He was a big, strong man. If I screamed, he would put his hand on my mouth—and things could get worse quickly.

I needed to think clearly.

I needed to think fast.

I needed to outsmart him.

His hand came to my breast, my thigh. I felt sick but pretended that I was starting to enjoy it, letting him continue until I was confident he thought I'd changed my mind. It was important for him to think that he had won me over, that I no longer wanted to fight or resist.

Then I told him I needed to use the toilet. By now he was happy, complacent, looking forward to his conquest. He got me my chair. As soon as I was in it, I pushed myself toward the door and unlocked it. For a moment, there seemed no option but to race along to the old, slow elevator at the end of the hall, but I was conscious that he could grab me and force me back to the room.

By pure good fortune, I heard the voices of some other guests.

This is my only chance.

I threw the door open and said loudly in Spanish that it had been nice meeting him, but that he must leave so that I could get up early in the morning. I was almost shouting. The other guests, I knew, couldn't fail to hear me.

My hope was simple enough—that he would be worried about what the other guests would think. I was giving him a way to leave and save face. If he cared about saving face, I could save myself.

Still speaking loudly, I thanked him for helping me.

"You must go," I told him. The tone of my voice, and the

look on my face, were intended to convince him that I wouldn't hesitate to yell "rape" if he didn't leave immediately.

He cursed me under his breath and left the room.

I locked the door and put several chairs and the bed by the door to barricade myself in. The light stayed on, and I watched for bugs, all the while knowing that he had tricked me with his terrifying tales about blood-suckers. It was me who had been the sucker.

What was I thinking? How did I ever let a strange man in my room?

In the morning, when I heard the sound of other guests on the floor opening their doors to catch the early bus back to San Jose, I removed the barricade and opened the door. I joined a middle-aged couple at the elevator and asked them to help me. They didn't realize that it wasn't porters I needed: it was a pair of bodyguards.

Never have I been so relieved to get on a bus.

I will never go back to this park.

I will never be this stupid again.

I will never be this stupid again.

And I was as good as my word—I haven't.

12.

Had there ever been anyone happier, freer, and more joyous than me? I was flying down a mountain, defying fate, defying what was "supposed" to be the end of a happy life at eighteen.

The colors of Chagall

Most of the time when I traveled, I was accompanied by a friend to help me over the curbs, or to share the problems that can arise when you're in unfamiliar places in a wheelchair.

Traveling alone in Europe was different. Five free weeks with a train pass that allowed me to decide which country or city to go to—as if the decision was as simple as deciding on the flavor of my next ice cream. There was an intensity about it that I loved.

A few minutes before I arrived in Nice, France, I began my ritual of asking a fellow passenger to help me get my chair and myself down from the train. It was the middle of the night.

"Excuse me, but I am getting off at the next stop and need some help getting my wheelchair. It's easy, and I'd really appreciate it—what do you think?"

"Well, I guess so, sure. Just tell me what I need to do."

The ritual successful, I happily alighted from the train. With so much practice, I had become an expert at selecting people who would help. They were usually surprised to see that I was traveling on my own—"shocked" might be a better word.

It was two in the morning and Nice was shrouded in darkness. It seemed forbidding, the train station being located in a part of town that I sensed was unsafe. Knowing the names of a few cheap places to stay from my *Let's Go* travel book, I pushed along the empty streets to find them. I felt vulnerable and was constantly looking over my shoulder to see whether anyone was following me, all the while trying not to let trepidation appear on my face or in my movements.

The first two lodging houses I tried didn't even open the door when I rang the doorbell. At one of them, a woman pushed back the window drapes and, upon seeing me, shook her head— *Non!*

I was sure it was because of the chair. I was frustrated, even a bit scared.

The next place, I decided, would be the one. Everything would be fine.

I rang the bell. By sitting on the steps, I was able to haul my wheelchair up close to the door so that when the owner opened it I'd be able to get inside quickly, before he slammed it shut.

"Excuse me, *excusez-moi*. Do you have any rooms available?" Suddenly, I regretted not having learned more French. It was clear that the proprietor did not speak English.

I made it inside. The lobby was old, musty and filthy. The paint on the wall was peeling off in large flakes. All the rooms were upstairs, and the elevator looked far too small to take my wheelchair.

What worried me most was the intimidating appearance of a guy leaning against the wall. He was in his mid-forties, short but muscular, with an overfed stomach hanging out of his tight blue T-shirt. Smoking a cigarette, he fixed me with a cold stare. He might have been a bouncer, but he could easily have passed as a serial killer. Something about him terrified me. Even so, going back outside seemed riskier than sleeping at this sleazy hotel. Through mime, I explained to the owner that I needed a room.

"Non," he replied. *"Non!"*

Soon, though, the owner realized that I wasn't going to leave, and that he had little alternative but to find somewhere for me to sleep.

I took out my money. He threw me a key and disappeared.

My next problem was maneuvering my wheelchair into a tiny elevator. Somehow, I needed to stand up and wedge it in beside me. The man in the blue T-shirt watched me icily, blowing rings of smoke.

This is not going to work, I thought.

The man made a move toward me. Whether he was coming to help me or hurt me I couldn't tell.

He signaled that I should use my canes to stand up in the elevator, and that he would bring my chair. On one hand, this seemed like an unexpected turn for the better. On the other hand, the thought of *him* following me up to my room sent shivers down my spine. My options were limited, so I took the elevator.

The man appeared grim-faced at the door of my room with my wheelchair. In actions and a torrent of French, he instructed me to lock my door. There was such insistence in his voice that I got the message loud and clear. I was in a dangerous location. Neither of us understood a word that the other was saying, but he also managed to communicate that I could call for help by using the telephone in my room.

The sheets on my bed had holes and smelled terrible. I kept my clothes on — my shoes and braces too, in case I needed to get out of there fast. A bare light bulb stayed on the whole night. My eyes remained open in anticipation of danger, every creak of the building seeming to warn of an intruder. I'd come to Nice to see the Marc Chagall museum but, right then, I couldn't wait to get back on a train.

Finally, daylight.

Outside, fresh air filled my lungs with relief. It was a new day. I pushed toward the Marc Chagall museum, knowing that the local buses didn't accommodate wheelchairs. Asking for directions, I learned that the museum was at the top of a steep hill and was offered a ride by a stranger. My first impulse was to decline, to politely explain that I'd be fine — but then I noticed he was wearing a brace, and had a dog in the back seat. *Good omens*, I thought.

At the museum I was surrounded by flying animals, strange beings and fantastic scenes from small Russian villages. It was wonderful. I felt elated and at home. Whatever it had taken to get there, it was worth it. I didn't want to leave.

Time slipped by and soon the museum was closing. It was hours until my train departed, so I flew down several miles of winding road in my wheelchair, reaching a wide boardwalk that lined the sea. The sun appeared through overcast skies and I felt confident again, with the sound of the waves keeping me company and magnificent Chagall images coloring my every thought.

I allowed the thrill of my independence to rise in me. *I am gliding around the world in my wheelchair!*

My mood froze as I met the chilling stare of the burly man

from the hotel. *It couldn't be*, I told myself. The chances of being in the same place at the same time in such a large city seemed impossible. Quickly I realized I was fooling myself. It was him, alright. There was no mistaking it.

It was him!

I was about to turn away, to push as fast as I could in another direction, when his face softened. A sparkle appeared in those vacant eyes and his hard, lined face melted into a shy smile.

I smiled back. He spoke to me rapidly in French. There was kindness in him, I could see it now. He had helped me with my wheelchair, and I hadn't noticed it even then.

I searched for something familiar in his words, hoping my Spanish would help me. Understanding came by degrees. He was speaking about his life as a sailor, his loneliness, and his philosophy of life. We talked, finding our way to an aquarium where he showed me his favorite fish. Then he showed me around his town, taking me through old flower markets and up the escalator in a crowded shopping center. A passing stranger would have taken us as old friends.

Somehow I was able to communicate to him that there were only a few more hours until my train left. He asked whether I was hungry. I said I was, and he signaled me to follow him.

We are going to his favorite restaurant, I thought.

We weren't. Soon we were in front of that awful hotel. Reluctantly, I followed him inside. He asked me to wait in the lobby for a few minutes, and went out again. I positioned myself by the door, on guard. Out of sheer curiosity, I waited. He returned ten minutes later with two large paper bags. Within minutes he had set a white tablecloth over an old pool table located just off the cramped lobby. Candles appeared, followed by bottled water and a bottle of red wine. He rushed past travelers in the lobby toward the kitchen, and re-emerged with a delicate mushroom omelet, small steaks, steaming potatoes and French bread.

I stared in amazement at this gourmet meal. As the candle flickered in that dimly lit room, he continued talking to me as though I were a long-lost friend. His eyes were twinkling. I understood enough to know that he was telling me of his lost youth and lost dreams, but the words didn't really matter.

It was the listening that mattered, and the moment.

Soft rain was falling as he walked me to the station. He helped me to board the train and instructed me to hide my money and passport, and not to talk to strangers. His kindness and concern made me want to reach out to him. I had judged him unfairly. He had acted with no impropriety. As he turned away, I grabbed his sleeve and pulled him toward me for a gentle hug. Embarrassed, he turned away quickly and disembarked from the train.

He stood on the platform, just outside my window. The train was delayed for over two hours with a mechanical problem, and he waited all that time. Occasionally he waved. He gestured that I should write. Several times I indicated that he should go home, but he just shook his head.

Finally, the train began to crawl out of the station. The man waved one last time, and his figure became smaller and smaller as the train increased its speed. I kept watching him, but still he didn't budge. The train took a turn, and then he was gone.

More than all the historic monuments and natural beauty and wonders I have seen in my frequent travels, this memory stayed with me. It remained vivid, forever wrapped in the magic and color of a Chagall painting. Was that because of the irony – the transformation of fear into friendship?

Perhaps that was part of it. I like to believe, however, that it was also about the transitory nature of life, its fleeting gifts, those rare moments when souls touch each other, all too briefly...

When I was eighteen, I thought of such encounters as "perfect moments", times when some life-force raises its head and tells us not to forget that we are alive.

Don't miss it, it will be gone soon.

Tuscany

The restaurant's name was "Belvedere". It seemed very quaint, and through its windows I could see rolling Tuscan hills and green valleys, where Italian villagers grew olives and grapes. Further away, there were glimpses of bright blue sea and the horizon.

It was almost noon, but I was the only customer. I had ordered *crostini* with olive oil, garlic and fresh tomato spread, followed by spaghetti, garlic chicken and *insalata mista*. I'd also ordered a glass of local wine, and tiramisu for dessert. It was a huge amount of wonderful food, and I could easily imagine I was shooting an Italian travel documentary featuring local cuisine. I was happy.

A man walked in. He was perhaps in his early sixties, with tousled gray hair and a beige overcoat that seemed a tad too large. His eyes were blue and contained a hint of mischief. Judging from the reaction of the waitress, he was a regular, taking his usual seat and ordering his usual meal. He gazed out the window, and I wondered what he was thinking.

Several times during the meal he looked at me, as if checking whether I was enjoying my meal and that all was well. He would smile, wink and then turn his attention back to his own plate, his private thoughts.

I thought about asking him to join me. Why should two people eat alone? Why not practice my Italian? For some reason, I decided against it. He seemed comfortable in his solitude, and we continued eating exchanging occasional friendly glances.

He finished his meal, wiped his mouth and gulped the last of his red wine. As he was leaving, he passed by my table.

"See you tomorrow," he said. "Same time, same place."

As he spoke, he reached out and squeezed my right breast.

My mouth flew open in disbelief. I was stunned, uncertain about how to react.

Was that a mistake? Did he mean to grab my arm instead?

In my astonishment, it occurred to me that the man might be one of those infamous Italian butt-pinchers, forced to improvise since I was always sitting on mine.

Same time, same place? No way, no how!

But the man had gone, leaving me to ponder again similarities between traveling alone and being in some surreal dream, with quirky, inexplicable moments that make boredom impossible.

I finished my meal and made my way through Castagneto Carducci, a medieval city with narrow, winding streets. Some of the streets were so steep that I often needed to ask local folks to help me down. By the time I reached the edge of the city, the shimmering blue sea was beckoning to me—even though it was more than seven kilometers away, down a long, winding road which had no shoulder for bikers or pedestrians, and which cars seemed to use as a racetrack.

Logic and safety awareness abandoned me. With my padded green cycling gloves on, I set out on the highway, braking with my hands as much as possible. Cars, trucks and motorcycles whizzed by me. Perplexed drivers stared at me in disbelief.

I didn't care.

I was flying. Faster and faster, maintaining control around dangerous curves but only barely, past olive groves and cows toward the sea. If one person had failed to see me on the road, it would have been the end of me.

I didn't care.

The wind plastered my hair back and my wheels hummed over the cement road.

Is there anyone happier, freer, and more joyous than me? I thought. *I'm in Italy, alone, flying down a mountain, defying fate, defying what was "supposed" to be the end of a happy life at eighteen.*

After making it safely to the ocean, I enjoyed a lovely meal with strangers at a seafood restaurant. My own meal finished, I ate their leftover dishes shamelessly. I conversed in the nearest I could get to Italian—my far-from-perfect Spanish masked by what I hoped was the right accent. I didn't worry about grammar or my tiny vocabulary. I mimed, I made up words—anything to connect with people. For me, that's the essence of traveling.

The next day I set out on the road inland for Siena, a walled city that has remained much as it was in the fifteenth century. It was getting close to Yom Kippur, the Day of Atonement, and I'd been told that there was a synagogue there, where the remnant of a once-large Jewish community gathered.

In Siena, however, the tourist office advised me that there were no rooms.

No wheelchair-accessible rooms, and no rooms—period.

But tomorrow, I explained, was Yom Kippur. "I am Jewish. For me, that's the holiest night of the year. I must be able to observe it and pray in the old synagogue."

It was no use. The woman told me to get a car or take a taxi to the next town. I was familiar with these kinds of situations, and told her that if she didn't find me a room I'd be sleeping in front of the door when she tried to close at the end of the day. I wasn't taking no for an answer—and she knew it.

We smiled at each other.

"Let's talk convents," I said. "Aren't there some nuns who would take me in? Nuns would understand how important it is for me to pray on Yom Kippur."

"*Prego.*"

She called a few convents, and eventually found one that had a room. I thanked her and pushed through the city for about half an hour, up steep hills and past gothic cathedrals. At the Santa Dominica convent, there was a staircase down to the entrance— about thirty or forty steps. Using my routine of getting out of my chair and asking someone to assist me down, I made it to the bottom with all my gear and was greeted by a screeching nun in full white headdress and traditional robes.

"How am I possibly going to manage?" It was a rhetorical question, yelled in Italian. She gestured inside. "There are steps everywhere here. I told the tourist office about them!"

Everything would be fine, I assured her. I'd manage

somehow. I wouldn't be any trouble. Finally, she let me check in and gave me a key. Still, however, she ranted. How could I do such a journey *solo*?

I was tired, too tired to hear a familiar speech about the problems and dangers inherent in traveling alone.

"There is no need to fear," I told her in my makeshift Italian. "I trust in God."

The nun's rapid-fire speech came to an abrupt halt.

She smiled.

13.

It has never been as if I'm striving to do what I used to be able to do – it's more about being happy with what I can do now, challenging myself with my body the way it is. It isn't a case of being half empty or half full – it is about loving my body whole.

A learning plan

In 1986, I was fortunate enough to be awarded a fellowship by the Kellogg Foundation. As part of this leadership program, I received funding for a "learning plan", giving me opportunities to creatively chart a course that would expand my horizons, skills and perspectives over a three-year period.

I did just that.

I lived in Spain and studied Spanish for a month in Salamanca. I went to South Africa for three weeks with a few other Kellogg Fellows, meeting with African National Congress (ANC) activists who were working fearlessly to end apartheid and reclaim their country. I participated in one of the first "citizen diplomacy" visits to Russia. I took a dance workshop in Vienna, learned how to ride dressage in Oregon, and cycled through China.

Like the Rotary Scholarship, the Kellogg Fellowship resembled a trampoline, launching me to the sky. I was exposed to new ideas and had journeys that I could never have imagined. Although I didn't realize it at the time, it would also provide me with the contacts I needed to change the lives of many disabled women throughout the world by developing a program to trampoline them, too, into leadership.

After my operation for syringomyelia, cycling had become a big part of my life, and the fellowship made it possible to explore the world even further. Cycling journeys took me back to France, where I rode past fairytale chateaux, and pastry shops where the aroma of coffee and chocolate croissants goes straight to your stomach. I went to Holland, where there are thousands of miles of *fiedspods*, bike paths where you never see any cars but pass windmills, dams, dikes, cows and the little towns where *appfelkuchen* pancakes lure you to cafés where you can sip hot chocolate and listen to the peal of church bells.

My friend Evelyn and I also went to China. She rented a bicycle and I sat in my wheelchair and hooked my two canes to its bike-rack, slipstreaming behind her. We rode through the crowded streets of Beijing, down narrow alleyways where people stared in absolute astonishment. Food was being cooked in front of their homes, essences of ginger and jasmine spicing the contents of cast iron pots. We rode into the countryside, past statues of Buddha, and arrived at small enclaves of chanting monks. Orange incense filled the air.

My travels have taken me from the most idyllic to the most horrific of places. In Sarajevo, I saw the Olympic stadium where thousands of Bosnians had been killed. I saw bullet-ridden homes, and stayed in a hotel with bullet-torn rugs. My view from a shattered window revealed missile-ravaged buildings and barbed wire fences where unexploded landmines were surrounded by multi-lingual warning signs.

I had visited Sarajevo with three other women with disabilities, advising people who wanted to organize beyond ethnic differences to demand accessibility when rebuilding their war-torn cities, and to demand access for disabled children through inclusive education. Though skeptical at first, the participants in our workshops eventually warmed to us—four feisty American women. They represented previously warring ethnic groups but were united by their disabilities—many inflicted by bombs, missiles or landmines—or by commitment to the interests of children with disabilities.

By the time we left, the mayor of the Bosnian city of Tuzla had signed a petition mandating that all new buildings be wheelchair-accessible—a notable victory for these people amidst much tragedy and despair. To my mind, though, we live in one world, so a step forward for some is good news for us all.

Refuseniks

In Russia, before Perestroika and the dismantling of the Soviet Union, I attended the "Women's March for Peace". Thousands of women paraded through the streets with flags, brightly colored banners and flowers. Perhaps because I was conspicuous in a long stream of able-bodied women, people from many countries ran up to me to give me their gifts—a little pen, an embroidered handkerchief.

We wanted to "peacen", or pacify, the world. There was

such optimism in the air. There were better ways, gentler ways, more humane ways. I was glad, and proud, to be part of the wave of change.

Before I left home, I had been asked by Jewish activists to contact some *refuseniks*—Jews who wanted to emigrate to Israel so that they could practice Judaism openly, but who were not permitted to leave the Soviet Union. I'd been warned that contacting these people was dangerous, that the *refuseniks* were watched by the secret police. Always prepared to take a risk, I had taken a list of contacts and their phone numbers, and the first person on the list was a single woman in her early thirties.

We met in a park. We talked.

We were followed by a man in a blue coat.

At first, I thought it was just my fertile imagination. It wasn't—and we both knew it.

"Oh, I'm used to it," she told me quietly.

I'm not, I thought, a little ashamed that I felt so scared.

The woman gave me some messages to pass on to her family in the USA, and I gave her some soap and other products that I knew she had wanted.

"Be careful, now that they have seen you with me, you may be watched too. Thank you so much for making contact with me. I feel so alone sometimes. It's good to know we are not forgotten. I'm praying that I will someday get my papers to go to Israel. Shalom."

We hugged and, before I could reply, she turned a corner and was gone.

But the man in the blue coat was not gone.

I turned a corner, he turned the corner.

I pushed faster, he walked faster.

Coincidence? Not likely!

I took one more corner, and he did the same. It was time to take action. I delved into the purple backpack hanging on the back of my wheelchair and grabbed for my Advil container, where I'd hidden the names and addresses of other *refuseniks* I had planned to visit.

Damn it, I thought. *I should have made copies of these names before I left my hotel room.*

I hadn't—and now this man, possibly a KGB agent, was following me.

I needed to destroy the list. Immediately.

I ripped the wrinkled piece of paper in half. I crumpled one half up into a little ball, popped it into my mouth and swallowed it. Trying to quickly muster some more saliva, I rolled up the other half of the list. With difficulty, I got it to slide down my throat. I pushed my chair to a nearby kiosk and drank a soda.

No sooner had I done this than I came face to face with the man in the blue jacket. My heart was pounding, but the list was gone.

What will he ask me? What will I say?

We eyeballed each other. Neither of us spoke. Then, as mysteriously as he had appeared, he disappeared into a white car that seemed to have been waiting for him.

I went cautiously through a park crowded with strolling families, back to my hotel. My head was spinning. I seemed to have stepped into a spy thriller, and then out again, all in the space of an hour.

No fear of flying

Tired arms. Hot, steaming water to soothe my muscles.

Exhilarating!

How many paraplegics have cycled along the green, windmill-lined paths of Holland, past medieval castles in France, or through crowded alleyways in China?

On many occasions, I've asked myself why travel has played such an important role in my life. Did I need rapid changes of scene to satisfy my restless mind? Was it because my dad spent fifteen years sailing the globe, and passed on an insatiable desire to experience the world not as part of a tourist package, but off the beaten track? His philosophy was similar to mine, best described by a saying attributed to an old monk: "Travel is a journey, and the journey is home."

Cycling and travel are such sensory experiences. The stimulation is constant. There's the smell of fresh-cut grass and cow dung in the warm air. There's the smell of the oil in woks on hot coals, cooking bok choy. There are unfamiliar sounds, and eye contact with strangers.

Perhaps I found cycling to be particularly invigorating because I was born athletic, and because I'm an incomplete paraplegic. The fact that I could move some of my leg muscles kept me at the edge of two worlds—not able-bodied enough to ride a bicycle without an extra wheel and a motor, yet capable of pedaling a little when the motor was running so that I could feel my quadriceps pumping. To me, the fluid movement of cycling didn't seem so very different from dancing, running—even flying!—and it made me feel alive. After a hot bath, my muscles felt like a plate of happy spaghetti, warm and relaxed.

The only way I could ride a regular bicycle was to get on the back of a tandem with a triangular kickstand to stabilize it when I was lifted on or off. I could, however, ride a horse alone as long it was trained to neck-reining and could respond to voice commands, and if there was a ramp or another form of assistance for mounting. For most disabled people nowadays, there are enough adaptations for you to be able to do almost anything—fly a plane with hand controls, ride a cycle with your arms, swing on a trapeze.

It has never been as if I'm striving to do what I used to be able to do—it's more about being happy with what I can do now, challenging myself with my body the way it is. It isn't a case of being half empty or half full—it is about loving my body whole, and enjoying my ability to have strong, fluid movements.

In my wheelchair, cycling, or riding a horse... I can fly.

14.

Under Chinese law no demonstrations were allowed. Yet here,
disabled women from all over the world were making a stand.
CNN cameras began rolling. Newspaper reporters scribbled
feverishly in their pads. The story was about to hit newspapers
and television screens all over the world.

Celebrating disability

"Today is the anniversary of my car accident. It occurred twenty-
four years ago."

A hush descended on the crowd—an awkward silence. The
room was filled with two hundred and fifty women with disabilities
from all over the world. The room was dotted with wheelchairs,
some old and boxy, others new and shiny, with no arm rests and
cambered wheels for sporting events. There were white canes on the
floor belonging to blind women. Brightly colored saris and other
traditional garments, some intricately woven, lit up an otherwise
dreary room. A group of Deaf women were sitting in the front row,
watching the sign language interpreter. There were also non-
disabled women, and many with disabilities that weren't
apparent— psychiatric survivors or women with learning
disabilities or epilepsy. It was hot, and there was the smell of sweet

sweat in the air. A tired old fan could be heard struggling against the odds, and rain was pounding the metal roof.

It was 29 August 1995. I was in Beijing, China, at the Fourth United Nations Conference and Non Government Organization (NGO) Forum on Women, and was addressing an international symposium on women with disabilities on the day before the start of the NGO Forum. To have helped organize such a symposium had been a dream. How ironic — or fitting — that it was occurring on August 29th, the same day as my car accident in Colorado. I was eighteen then. Now, I was forty-two.

I sensed that people were feeling sad, realizing that the accident I had referred to was the one that put me in a wheelchair. But that wasn't the sentiment I wanted to convey. After a slight pause I continued.

"But today is not a sad day for me. No — not at all. Today is a celebration. Yes, a celebration! I am celebrating that I am a woman with a disability. A proud woman with a disability. I am honored to be part of a wonderful global family of sisters. I am happy that we are finally coming together to celebrate and develop strategies so that the entire world will notice that we are loud, proud and passionate, and that we want to have our rights!"

There was another moment of silence as my words were translated into Spanish, French, Chinese, Arabic and Japanese. The sign language interpreters, interpreting in these same languages, were working hard to keep up with the rapid pace.

Then, as the sounds of translation subsided, there was resounding applause. Deaf women applauded by raising their hands in the air. The feeling was unanimous — this was a joyous and historic day.

Yet this was not only the best of times – it was also the worst of times.

The forum preceding the official UN conference was attended by thousands of women who worked for non-government organizations. It was held in Huairou, one and half hours outside Beijing, where the conference was taking place and where our hotel was located. We boarded non-accessible buses early in the morning by means of steep, makeshift ramps. Once we arrived in Huairou there were inaccessible streets and curbs that needed to be overcome. It rained, and there was mud everywhere. No sign language interpreters were provided at any of the sessions. Information was not available in Braille or on tape, leaving visually impaired women constantly having to ask others to read out printed information.

Despite a year of letter writing to the organizers of this huge event, the needs of disabled women had been ignored.

Maybe they thought we wouldn't really come?

Maybe it was too easy to blame the Chinese government for their own shortcomings?

Maybe they didn't really care?

At that time, disabled women's rights were not considered part of women's rights. Later, in a famous speech, Hillary Clinton would coin the phrase "Women's rights are human rights". Very true – but what about the rights of 250 million women with disabilities? Where were they? Who was listening?

We had expected things to be different in China, but hadn't really known *how* different. When our delegation of about fifty women with disabilities from the United States arrived at the airport, tired and worn from a twenty-hour journey, we had headed toward an elevator to avoid the hundreds of steps needed to access customs and passport control offices. We had been stopped by Chinese officials, who indicated that we needed to use the stairs or the escalator. For some security reason that no one could understand, the elevator was out of the question.

"But we are in wheelchairs, and have canes and crutches, and are exhausted," we pleaded.

In the USA we would have yelled and screamed. We'd have threatened to sue, organized a protest, called the media. We realized that none of these tactics were options. The stern faces of armed police who didn't speak much English were not to be moved. The officials could not have cared less.

"You are in China now, and you must follow regulations."

In shock, we sat on our rear ends and edged down the stairs. We maneuvered large wheelchairs, four women per chair. We did what we had to do.

This was going to be a whole new experience, where the notions of individual rights and disability rights did not carry any weight.

Solidarity

Although the Chinese experience was exhilarating in some ways — particularly the thrill of meeting women from all around the world — the inaccessibility of buildings and transportation was mentally and physically draining for us all. Women had worked hard to raise money to get there and began to complain about the buses, the venues, the food and hardships. Some became sick.

Tensions became obvious. This was not what we had expected. An accumulation of negative experiences began to simmer like hot water in a full kettle, and threatened to boil over.

Soon, something snapped.

One of the workshops in the NGO Forum was on disabled women's issues. When the presenters went to find the workshop room early in the morning to prepare for their session, they were shocked to find that the room was on the third floor. There was no elevator.

How could that happen? Could things get any worse?

Who would have thought that a workshop about disability issues would be held in an inaccessible building?

It was unbelievable.

The women gathered in front of the building, shaking their heads and shouting. When the news spread, others joined them. They began to chant in a circle. A spontaneous protest was erupting, and non-disabled women added to the numbers. The momentum increased.

Very quickly, the media got the whiff of a story. Under Chinese law, no demonstrations were allowed. People were forbidden from congregating for political reasons, yet here, disabled women from all over the world were making a stand. CNN cameras began rolling. Newspaper reporters scribbled feverishly in their pads. The days of meek, passive disabled women were gone. This story was about to hit newspapers and televisions all over the world.

A plan was agreed on. We would infiltrate the conference by bringing the issues of disabled women to every session held. No matter whether the subject was health policy, education or domestic violence, some of our two hundred and fifty women with disabilities would be there, voicing our concerns. After the media frenzy subsided, the women dispersed to implement our plan.

What we didn't know was that somewhere, another plan was being formed. Although this could never be substantiated, it seems clear that the Chinese authorities wanted to punish us for our demonstration. That evening, we were told by the conference organizers that no buses would be available for our group the next day. No buses—and no reason given as to why. Mere coincidence? I don't think so.

I was appalled. How could they? With no transportation, we were completely stranded. Cindy, my close friend and one of the coordinators of the disabled women's symposium, was equally horrified. What could we do?

After much inquiry, we learned that a high-level planning meeting was to be held that night. It would be attended by senior representatives of the NGO Forum and some Chinese Government officials. We decided to make an appearance, and soon I was again delivering an impassioned speech. I explained the frustration caused by the inaccessible workshop venue for our workshop, as well as all the other barriers that women with disabilities were facing in Beijing and Huairou. I cried, and needed tissues. Exhaustion helped make the scene more dramatic, which probably worked in our favor.

"You *must* give us our buses back," I said.

The room remained quiet as I pleaded our case. When I was finished, I was told to wait outside with Cindy. A van would be provided to transport us back to our hotel. There was no indication of what the verdict would be.

As furious as we were, I was also scared. We were seen as the leaders of a disabled women's conspiracy that had caused trouble for the organizers and international shame for China. What would they do to us? We were not in a place where American laws protected us.

Then, just as I was feeling most vulnerable, the strangest thing happened. We were waiting for the promised van when a dignified looking man asked us whether we were hungry. It was almost midnight, and Cindy and I had missed dinner. *Of course* we were hungry.

I expected some simple rice and perhaps some bok choy or other vegetable, which would have suited us fine. I was surprised that they had offered us anything after taking away our group's transportation.

It was a balmy night. As we waited for our meals on a warm balcony, we were informed that the man who had approached us was the Mayor of Huairou. Appetizers appeared — not just ordinary appetizers but gourmet dumplings and other delicacies. Then, just as we thought our delicious treat was over, several women arrived bearing more fabulous dishes. A banquet was in store for us — but why? What did it mean? If the goal of the Chinese was to baffle us, it was working!

Our buses arrived the following morning, and the threat to withdraw them was never discussed again. Nevertheless, strange things continued to occur. Whenever Cindy and I met with a few disabled women outside the hotel, or in the lobby, a man would suddenly appear and take our photos with a big camera and a bright flash — as if to intimidate us by letting us know that we were being watched. Our faxes were being read and our phone conversations were being listened to. It was clear that our "shadows" knew what we were doing and where we were going, and they could not have known otherwise.

Once, when Cindy and I took a cab to get some passes for the rest of the group to attend some special ceremonies, the driver pulled over and told us to get out. We begged him to continue.

"Get out of the taxi? Why? We are in the middle of nowhere! Why won't you take us to our destination. We will never find another cab out here!"

"You must leave. I have been instructed that I cannot take you any further."

Our questions and pleas got us nowhere. Out we got. Cindy took my wheelchair from the trunk. We crossed a huge street and, after much difficulty, managed to find and convince another taxi to take us further.

Day after day, there was more of the same: rainy days, potholes filled with muddy water, complaints, frustrations. Exhausted and outraged, some disabled women held Cindy and me, as organizers of the symposium that had brought so many women with disabilities to Beijing, responsible for their hardships.

Cindy, who was not disabled, was assumed by everyone from hotel staff to conference officials to be the boss, a role she didn't want. Was it *that* difficult for them to believe that Cindy's boss was the woman with the wheelchair, descending stairs on her rear end and being bounced around on buses?

Yet, despite the problems, the seed for the international disabled women's movement had been sown. Solidarity was nurtured. We asked disabled women from other nations what they wanted in the future. They told us it was leadership training, and the chance to meet other disabled women and share stories, traumas, hopes and skills. They wanted to learn how to get the power and funding to make changes for disabled women and girls in their communities. Cindy and I listened and, from this time, began to formulate what would become a signature MIUSA program: the Women's Institute on Leadership and Disability (WILD).

We knew, too, that our message was being noticed. Madeleine Albright, then United States Secretary of State, visited the disabled women's tent and heard of our hopes and frustrations. Cindy was asked by Judy Heumann, a powerful disability rights activist who was part of the official US delegation, to confer with speech writers for US First Lady Hillary Clinton. A sentence was inserted into Ms. Clinton's speech acknowledging the presence of women with disabilities at this historic conference.

The trip took its toll on us, and I got sick and developed such a fever that I imagined I had contracted some sort of exotic killer virus. I felt sure the Chinese government was out to physically harm us, but Cindy nursed me back to health. We had originally planned to visit Hangzhou, a beautiful bucolic city where we had friends who were part of the budding Chinese disability rights movement, but we cancelled that part of the trip, no longer feeling safe for ourselves, or for the friends we planned to visit. Paranoia was setting in. By the end of two weeks, we were fatigued to the point of dizziness and more than ready to go home.

One final drama awaited us when we tried to get earlier flights back home.

"All the flights are booked."

In tears, Cindy blurted out our dramatic story and, by some

miracle, the airline representative from United Airlines happened to be from Oregon. Hearing we were alumni of the University of Oregon, he became nostalgic and found us two tickets home. We were upgraded to business class, where more leg room and better food awaited us. But we just couldn't relax. Tired though we were, the stress had been too great.

As the plane landed in the United States, I took a big breath and heaved a sigh of relief. I thought my difficulties were over. In truth, they were only beginning.

My parents had decided to move from New York to Eugene. I had no idea how significantly my life was about to change.

15.

When I emerged from the house for the first time, symbolically re-entering the world of the living, the sky was gray. A group of clouds separated, and for a moment a few rays of sunshine streamed down from the sky. Almost as quickly, the gap closed and the rays were gone. It was my dad saying goodbye to me.

Place of two speeds

My mom and dad found a lovely apartment on the other side of the river from my house in Eugene.

"Gan Eden," my dad said, using the Hebrew for Garden of Eden. "This place is so beautiful!"

In the past, he had teased that Eugene was a town with only two speeds—slow and stop. It was a joke but there was a kind of truth in it for him. He was used to the frenetic pace of life in New York, Broadway shows, famous museums, an endless variety of ethnic restaurants. I had been surprised when he said he wanted to move to semi-rural Eugene.

"I want to be closer to you," he had said when I questioned him about his decision on the phone.

I knew that was true, but I also felt there was more to it. Something was happening with my mom. She was changing. There were signs that we found difficult to read — in her moods, her personality, her mind. I had seen them, and my dad had seen them too. He didn't know what was going on, but his intuition made him certain that it was a big change, something he wouldn't be able to handle by himself. He needed my help.

Maybe — just maybe — he had another intuition too.

Eugene. For him, it was a place of two speeds.

There was slow.

And there was stop.

Honoring my parents

I returned from Beijing a few months before Rosh Hashanah, the Jewish New Year. Although weary, it felt great to be home and I enjoyed being so close to my parents for the first time since I left New York after rehab. There was also some exciting news for me, and I was thrilled to be able to share it with my mom and dad.

I had been chosen as Disabled American of the Year, now known as the President's Award. I was to be honored in the Oval Office at the White House and presented with the award by President Bill Clinton. It was amazing, and most of all I was happy for my parents. As the daughter of two immigrants who didn't finish high school, I knew what it would mean to them. They had started their lives all over again in a strange new land after surviving the Holocaust. They had lost their mothers, fathers, sisters and brothers in the most horrific ways. They had suffered with me after my car accident and they had given me strength. Now I could somehow honor them for all they had been through. I would bring them to the White House to meet the President, and I would honor them through this prestigious award.

I read them the invitation letter sent from the Executive Office of the White House. We sat outside their new apartment, hearing the rush of the river. The sky was a brilliant blue, and the air was full of birdsong. My parents listened closely, concentrating on each and every word. They smiled proudly. I read the letter slowly, and they said nothing. In the pauses, we just sat, as if capturing the purity of our togetherness.

I noticed a lone bird, with a long wingspan, circling above the water. It seemed to be missing its partner. It looked lost and was searching. I looked away, but had taken it in with a sense of foreboding.

Unbearable

I went back to work at MIUSA and was preparing to fly to Washington DC at around 6.00 a.m. the next day.

"Susan there's a phone call for you."

I was sitting at my desk, and it was about 4.30 p.m.

It was Tom, telling me about my father.

My dad had collapsed. Unconscious, he was being rushed to hospital. I remember nothing else that Tom said, and don't even remember getting in my car and driving to the hospital. Some other mechanism seemed to take over.

When I arrived at the emergency room, my dad had regained consciousness and was happy to see me, but the nurses were still working frantically on him.

"Did I have a stroke?" he asked.

"No. You had a heart attack, but you're going to be fine."

"Susan. You need to go to Washington to get your award."

"I'm not going without you. I want you to get better."

I was in shock. How could this be happening?

The time that followed became one big blur. My father spent several days in hospital but seemed to be doing fine. He was his old, charming self, making conversation with everyone he met. Having never taken a sick day in his life, it was all such a new experience for him. Doctors talked to me as if I was his wife. My mom listened, but seemed glad that I could take charge.

Eventually he was allowed to go home, and we started to get into a routine of attending follow-up appointments. My award ceremony at the White House was postponed, and my dad received a personal letter from President Clinton wishing him a fast recovery. I spent as much time with my parents in their apartment as I could, making sure that my dad got plenty of rest. I inhaled the scent of his Paco Rabanne cologne. His eyes still twinkled and I couldn't get enough of them. I locked an image of them into a special place in my memory. Perhaps, at some sub-conscious level, I knew that I needed to.

Two weeks later, I was with a group of disabled teenagers on an exchange program organized by MIUSA. They were from Russia, and I was escorting them through a neighborhood school, discussing inclusive education. I was feeling anxious, distracted. I didn't know why.

Then I received a call.

My father.

My dad.

When I got to the hospital, he could see me but couldn't speak. He looked at me with frightened eyes. He'd had a major stroke.

For three days I stayed at his bedside while he slipped away. I cried, and he managed to wipe my tears and hold my hand. We both knew what was happening and — in the intensive care ward — they told me he wouldn't recover. The thought was unbearable.

I leaned over his bed. Urine was running down my leg because I was afraid that if I used the bathroom he'd be gone when I returned. I called my Rabbi. Tom, the Rabbi and I sang Hebrew songs, surrounding him with what we knew he loved most. The end was near.

His breathing stopped.

I asked for some time alone with him. I said my goodbyes and kissed him as many times as I could through my endless flow of tears, still needing the touch of his skin.

I left the hospital with my mom and Tom. We were numb.

The funeral arrangements needed to be made.

Rays of sunshine

"Where was your father educated?"

The funeral director had a million questions to ask for his documentation.

"He went to *cheder* in Podwoloczyska. It's like *Yeshiva...*"

I could see that the funeral director had no idea what I was talking about. He repeated the question, seemingly devoid of any genuine human emotion. Couldn't he see the trauma we were experiencing?

"My father graduated from Harvard with a PhD," I told him.

The funeral director was satisfied with this, and recorded the information. Somewhere in the bureaucracy, the statistics were going to be skewed but I didn't care. My mind and body were in another zone.

The Jewish religion has beautiful and wise traditions for dealing with death. We sat *shiva* for seven days, never leaving the house, surrounded by friends who brought food and comfort. We chanted the Kaddish daily.

When I emerged from the house for the first time, symbolically re-entering the world of the living, the sky was gray. A group of clouds separated, and for a moment a few rays of sunshine streamed down from the sky like a ladder. Almost as quickly, the gap closed and the rays were gone.

It was my dad saying goodbye to me.

I continued to push around the block, warm tears streaming down my face.

The Oval Office

Six months later, I went to Washington DC to receive my award from the President. I invited my neurosurgeon friend, Dr. Gene Bolles, along with my mom and Tom. I wished my father could be there and cried a lot, especially in the hours waiting to see the President.

In the Oval Office, Bill Clinton showed the charisma and

personal charm he was famous for.

My mom said loudly: "Bill, you are even more good-looking and charming than I thought!" Everyone burst out laughing, including the President. It broke the somber mood.

I knew my dad was watching. Up in the clouds, or perhaps standing right next to me, he was proud.

Pumpkins

The night before my dad had his stroke, we had carved pumpkins in his apartment. It was the first time he'd ever done such a thing. It wasn't a Jewish tradition but I had always carved pumpkins when I was a child, and had gone "trick or treating" with the other kids. It had been part of my assimilation into a non- Jewish society.

On that October night before everything changed, my dad had a glint in his eye. He was like a little boy, innocent and playful.

Every year now, when the autumn chill arrives and the pumpkins appear, I feel a terrible sadness. I can no longer carve pumpkins, or have them in my house. When I see them, I know that the anniversary of my father's death is approaching.

November would continue to host momentous events for me, always juxtaposing the good with the bad. Who knows why?

The book of life

First and foremost, we are Jewish. That is our heritage, our source, our soul.

For many years I traveled from Oregon to New York to sit by my father for Rosh Hashanah services. It felt like home. Since I was very young I had taken my place beside him at the synagogue, listening to his proud voice, singing with uncompromised emotion in Hebrew, his first language. My dad would greet people as they entered the synagogue and walked past our seats, almost as if he were hosting a tribal gathering. I played with the ends of his *tallis*, the traditional blue-and-white prayer shawl, and joined him in singing our special Hebrew songs.

When I was older, and used a wheelchair and two canes, he carried my wheelchair up and down the steep flights of stairs. I walked slowly and cautiously with my canes, laboring over each step as I wondered why money had been spent on lavishly redecorating the main hall instead of installing an elevator.

I also wondered why it was only men who led the prayers. I once told my dad that I would dress up like Yentl in the Barbara Streisand movie, so I could look like a boy and have an *aliyah* – a reading of the sacred Torah – with him. My father agreed that females should have such rights and encouraged me to do it. We both knew I was joking, but I understood that what my dad said reflected his true values.

After my parents moved to Oregon to be closer to me, we would sit together more regularly in the synagogue in Eugene, where there were no steps but a ramp to the *bimah*, the raised platform where the Torah is kept. By then, there were women rabbis, and gay marriages had been embraced.

Before my father died, I was given perhaps one of the greatest Jewish honors and invited to give the Yom Kippur speech. With my *tallis* draped proudly over my shoulders, I addressed hundreds of people, with my Dad and Mom in the first row.

During the Yom Kippur service, it is the tradition in our synagogue to gather as a family under a *tallis*, held above our heads by the tallest person with outstretched arms. The shawl forms a kind of tent, cocooning us and each of the other families as we huddle together and hold each other singing special prayers. Being a tradition not practiced by more conservative synagogues, this was slightly amusing to my father.

"So this is Oregon," he whispered to me once, grinning mischievously. "Are they afraid it's going to rain?"

We smiled at each other. I held my daddy close, cherishing the moment and contemplating the awe of the holiday season, which acts as a solemn reminder that we do not know who will be inscribed next in the *sefer chaim*, the Book of Life.

16.

I went out to the hallway and then down the stairs, asking someone to assist with my chair. At the bottom of the steps, I cried out loud. I hadn't wanted to obey the rabbi, but at the same time his attitude made me no longer want to remain in his presence.

Discrimination

Some months after my father's death, I was given an all-expenses paid trip to Singapore by Rotary International to receive an Alumni Achievement Award for the work I had accomplished for disabled people since I received my Rotary Scholarship to study in Australia.

I felt honored, and Tom and I soon discovered that Singapore has no shortage of delicious food. One night, after eating more than twenty delicately wrapped Peking duck rolls at an all-you-can-eat buffet, we went on a tour of the zoo. It was exciting to see exotic animals wandering around in darkness, with only a few carefully placed lights enabling us to glimpse their nocturnal world. I also held hands with a furry orangutan, whose dark, sad eyes were hauntingly human-like. His slender fingers grasped my hand like a small child. It was magical.

On a Friday night, however, I found myself sobbing.

Everything was marvelous, yet I could not stop crying.

I was looking for a synagogue so that I could say Kaddish, just as I had every week since my father's death. I hadn't missed any opportunity to recite this prayer, which I knew so well in Hebrew, because it not only honored my dad but also gave me a few moments to connect with his presence in the sanctity and comfort of a synagogue, a place he regarded as home. Although I had guessed that there would only be a small Jewish community in Singapore, I'd been confident of finding a synagogue and saw it as a way of sharing the Alumni Achievement Award with my dad.

Finally, I found Singapore's one and only synagogue — but my relief was mixed with frustration. There were at least twenty steps leading up to the entrance. I shouldn't have been surprised, however, because as much as I loved Judaism I was often appalled that so many synagogues were without ramps, and had inaccessible bathrooms and *bimahs*.

Sizing up those twenty steps, I remembered an incident from my childhood. It was at Hebrew school, and someone had asked me what I wanted to do when I grew up.

"I want to be a rabbi," I responded proudly.

I loved Hebrew school, which I attended three afternoons a week after public school for five years. Unlike many other kids, I loved singing the prayers. It was wonderful learning both modern and ancient Hebrew, understanding the rituals and holidays, and receiving the wise teachings. Why *wouldn't* I want to become a rabbi?

"You mean a *rebbitzin*," an older woman who taught at the Hebrew school corrected.

This was a word I'd never heard before.

"What's a *rebbitzin*?" I asked.

"It's the rabbi's wife. Women don't become rabbis in the conservative or orthodox Jewish religion. But you would make a wonderful *rebbitzin* I'm sure."

Rabbi's wife? I thought. No, thanks! I want to be the rabbi. If I can't be the rabbi, forget it. The very next day, I dropped out of Hebrew high school, a continuation of Hebrew school for those who wanted to pursue Jewish studies after their Bat Mitzvahs.

The huge climb I faced in Singapore revived those feelings of exclusion. I had experienced them as a female, and now, as a disabled person, I felt doubly unwelcome. Yet my desire to say Kaddish for my dad was too strong to let this defeat me. I asked Tom to carry my wheelchair up the steps, and then struggled with my canes and shaky legs to ascend the steps, stopping to sit and rest several times.

It wasn't a very dignified way to begin the Sabbath, but I told myself to put this out of my mind and let nothing dampen the joy I felt about making my parents proud. I knew my mom, back in Eugene, was feeling great *nachas* (pride for a loved one's achievements) and I went into the synagogue ready to share some special moments with my father. Exhausted from the *shlep* up, I found a seat at the back of the synagogue in the very last row.

Within moments, the cantor approached me.

"I'm sorry, but you must sit upstairs with the rest of the women and girls," he said rather sheepishly. "This is an orthodox synagogue."

Orthodox synagogues are the strictest in their adherence to ancient rules and regulations, and impose *mechitsa* — a separation of men and women during prayer. Sometimes, there is even a large curtain between the men and the women, sitting on different sides of the synagogue. Sometimes, too, the women and girls are required to sit upstairs—and this was the case in Singapore. In a city with one synagogue, what was I supposed to do? I couldn't go to the next suburb and find a conservative or reform synagogue, could I?

I looked across at the steep, narrow, winding staircase that led to the balcony. These were not just any stairs. They were a barrier I could not cross.

"That's impossible," I said, still catching my breath after my climb up the steps outside. "I just can't go up any more steps. I understand that you separate men and women, and—although I don't agree with that personally—I respect that you and this congregation are orthodox and it's your custom. But this is also the only Jewish place of worship in Singapore, so all Jews must come here to pray. Would it be okay if I sit here, in the very back row, where no one is sitting? I'm here to recite Kaddish for my father."

The cantor must have seen the worn look on my face. He thought for a moment and then nodded. When he walked to the front to begin the service, he and the rabbi seemed to have a bit of a discussion about it, but soon the service began. I relaxed and began singing the prayers, finally feeling a little at home—as all Jews should feel when they enter a synagogue anywhere in the world, part of a family unified by our Hebrew language and rituals.

I was deep in prayer, almost in a trance, when I noticed that the rabbi was walking toward me - or at least toward the back of the synagogue. Since everyone was praying, I thought it unusual that he should be leaving the *bimah* where he'd been leading the service with the cantor.

It was definitely me he was heading for. He came up to me,

leaned over and whispered in my ear.

"You must go upstairs with the other women. You may not pray here. This is an orthodox synagogue."

"I know this is an orthodox synagogue, but I can't go up any more steps. I already had to *shlep* up the steps to get in here, but I physically can't do any more. I'm not bothering anyone here—the back row is empty. The cantor said it was okay."

I hoped that would end the discussion, so that we could both go back to doing what we had come to do.

"I'm sorry," he continued. His tone was adamant. "You must go upstairs. You are too distracting to those of us praying."

Distracting? I thought. *That really doesn't make sense. Surely you are the one causing a distraction. You are certainly distracting me from my prayers!*

He demanded that I move. The rabbi wasn't taking no for an answer.

"I can't," I replied.

"Well, then, you will have to go out into the hallway, outside the doors of the sanctuary."

I was already shocked, but now I was becoming furious.

"You want me to pray in the hallway? I came here to say Kaddish for my dad. I refuse to do that in the hallway. My father's family was murdered in the Holocaust. These were people who would rather be killed than be denied the practice of Judaism, and you are throwing me, my father's daughter, into the hallway because I'm paraplegic and can't go up a huge winding staircase? Do you have any idea how insulting and disrespectful that is?"

It appeared that he wasn't affected at all by my speech.

"And do *you* have any idea how insulting and disrespectful

you are being to the customs of the orthodox synagogue you have entered? This is our house of worship. We have our customs and you need to respect them. Please go out into the hallway."

I didn't know what to do. This man was not about to change his mind. I couldn't argue any longer because tears were welling in my eyes, and my throat was jammed with a lump of wailing and sobbing just waiting to be unleashed.

Soon the tears started flowing and there was no way of stopping them. I went out to the hallway and then down the stairs, asking someone to assist with my chair. At the bottom of the steps, I cried out loud. I hadn't wanted to obey the rabbi, yet at the same time his attitude made me no longer want to remain in his presence.

When the service was over, people poured out of the synagogue. The cantor looked embarrassed when he saw me, and apologized. I asked him to bring my chair up the steps into the empty synagogue so that I could at least say Kaddish. He assisted me, and again apologized for the actions of the rabbi.

Afterwards, Tom and I went back to our hotel. I cried all the way.

I cried because I missed my dad.

I cried because I knew my father would have been horrified by the treatment I had received.

I cried for having this night spoil my joyous trip.

I cried for all the other people who didn't go to synagogues because the steps and bathrooms seemed to scream: *You are not welcome here!*

I cried because, as a woman, I had been made to feel inferior.

The discrimination I had experienced assailed all aspects of my identity, touching every part of me that made me proud of who

I am: being Jewish, being a woman, and being disabled. It was all too much to bear.

The next day, we left on our scheduled flight back to Eugene.

Praying for change

Many years later, at a Passover *seder*, I told my Singapore story.

Today, in the United States, there are women rabbis in both the reform and conservative movements of Judaism—though not in orthodox synagogues—and I could have grown up to be a rabbi, not just a *rebbitzin*. Women rabbis are re- interpreting the ancient texts using a feminist paradigm.

Today, too, synagogues are making entrances and bathrooms wheelchair accessible, and there are programs so that anyone can have a Bar or Bat Mitzvah, including those with learning disabilities or Down's Syndrome. Some synagogues conduct services in sign language.

"Susan, that was one orthodox rabbi – and what he did was wrong. I'm so sorry that happened to you."

This was the response of an old friend, a ninety year-old man who attended the orthodox synagogue in Eugene.

I thought, I pondered. So many years I had carried this story with me. At that *seder*, I let the hurt flow out of me.

Someday I will return to that synagogue in Singapore. Maybe there will be a ramp, and I will be welcomed.

Now *that's* something to pray for—and to work for, too.

Rosh Hashanah in Vietnam

One year after my father's death, I was in Vietnam. I was facing my first Rosh Hashanah without him.

"You're going *where*?"

My friends were astonished. Rosh Hashanah and Vietnam seemed an improbable match.

I'd been invited to be a part of a high level delegation studying disability programs and policy in Vietnam. I dreaded sitting at the synagogue in Eugene missing my dad, knowing that the raw wound of loss and grief had formed only the thinnest of scabs, and that I'd be overcome with sadness. Vietnam had sounded like an oasis, an escape. I could be by myself and have my own religious service in a private, introspective way. If I could find some fellow Jews—probably away from home, like me—I would join them and see what paths had led them to the celebration of Rosh Hashanah in Vietnam. When I learned that our delegation would be in Hue, a small city between Hanoi and Ho Chi Minh City (formerly Saigon), that possibility became more remote.

I packed my *siddur* (prayer book) and the traditional *shofar* (ram's horn) in my backpack as I prepared to do Rosh Hashanah solo. I wasn't sure that the *shofar* would get through customs, but it did.

As the plane prepared to land in Ho Chi Minh City, I could see from the window the beautiful pastoral landscape of a country that I had previously only seen from my living room, with horrific scenes of napalm, death and destruction. Fields of rice lay below, water shimmering in the early morning light. Farmers were harvesting their crops. Here and there I could see buffaloes dragging plows.

We were driven through the city and I saw people with disabilities—many amputees from the war—sitting on dirt floors hammering scrap metal to make small implements, barely making a living. I went to elegant receptions at the US embassy, attended by military officials who had once stood at the helm of opposing armies. I visited serene Buddhist monasteries. At one of these, I saw an old blue car that had been used by a monk from Hue who had been featured on the cover of *Time* magazine after driving to Saigon, drenching himself in kerosene and setting himself aflame as a protest against the war and the treatment of Buddhists.

All these scenes I observed with my *siddur* and *shofar* in my pack, hung over the back of my wheelchair. They were objects too holy to be left on a shelf in some hotel room, and through them I kept my father's spirit close. Even so, the thought of living through the High Holy Days of Rosh Hashanah without him seemed almost too much to bear.

After boarding the plane from Ho Chi Minh City to Hue, I took out my *siddur* and turned to the prayers for the High Holy Days. I was determined to recite the entire service, using whatever time I had, and the plane was as good a place as any. I had taken my seat first, as wheelchair users do, and had barely begun reading when other passengers started boarding.

To my surprise, I heard Hebrew. Not just a *shalom* or two, but whole conversations—chitchat, questioning and joking.

In Hebrew!

At first, I thought I was dreaming—but it rapidly became clear that the flight's passenger list included a group of about twenty-five Israelis. One after the other, they filed down the narrow aisles.

A woman stopped near my seat and, struggling to fit her bag into the overhead compartment, caught my eye.

"Is that a prayer book?" She asked in English.

"Yes," I replied, still gaping a little at the mind-boggling fact that a party of Israelis had boarded my flight just as I'd started reading my *siddur*. "What are all of you doing here?"

"We are on a study tour of Asia, looking at ancient temples and learning about the history. And you?"

I told her of my involvement with the disability rights delegation, and explained how we were working with the Vietnamese government to share ideas and information about legislation.

"What are you going to do for Rosh Hashanah?"

"I don't know exactly," I replied, showing her my *shofar*.

Soon she was loudly announcing to all her tour mates on the plane how strange and wonderful it was to find an American in Vietnam reciting the Rosh Hashanah prayers in Hebrew, with her *shofar*. The sound of Hebrew filled the plane. There was laughter, and there was the shared awe of finding others from our tribe in such a situation.

"You must join us for Rosh Hashanah in our hotel," I was told.

And I did.

In the middle of Hue, I sat with twenty-five Israelis celebrating Rosh Hashanah. It was surprising, and it was delightful. Our hotel hosts made a traditional Vietnamese feast, accompanied by an elderly lute player. They also provided colorfully embroidered Vietnamese robes and hats. Perhaps something had been lost in translation when the Israeli tour leaders asked for a banquet to celebrate their special day?

With *yarmulkas* (prayer coverings) on our heads and wearing our Vietnamese robes, we ate the traditional yellow honey cake and gefilte fish—which my companions had carried with them from Israel—as well as a variety of Vietnamese delicacies. As the only one to have carried a *shofar* across the world, I was called upon to blow it, and we sang many Hebrew songs.

I cried tears of happiness.

My sweet, kind father, I thought. *You surely arranged this for me from heaven.*

Dr. Binh

The trip to Vietnam continued to be magical.

The man who had organized it was a quadriplegic. An ex-marine, he had a spinal cord injury as a result of a bullet wound received in Hue during the Vietnam War. Since then, he had become a disability rights activist. We accompanied him to a field, the exact location where he had been shot. Amazingly, an old, toothless peasant woman remembered him, and the battle that had occurred that day.

Later, when I was wandering around outside my hotel looking for insect repellant, another magical connection occurred. I saw a man in sandals, who appeared to be a local, and decided to ask for help. Assuming he didn't speak English, I mimed with great dramatic flair the scene of a mosquito biting my arm.

"Bzzzzzzz... bugs... bite.... bite ... Ow! I buy?"

"Oh, you are looking for mosquito repellant?"

I was astonished. His English was perfect. His name, I discovered, was Dr.Binh, and he was dean of the Hue Medical School, specializing in pediatrics. He was in charge of hundreds of young medical students learning about rural health care.

We became instant friends. I shared books I had brought with me about children with disabilities, and about low cost ways to bring health care and rehabilitation to disabled children. Dr. Binh talked to me about the challenges disabled people face in Vietnam.

One of my favorite moments came when we were sharing a taxi to visit some rural villages where there were many children with cerebral palsy. When I saw a bumble bee in the car, I was immediately afraid of being stung. I must have seemed quite panicky, so Dr. Binh gently cornered the angry bee, wrapped it in a tissue and released it outside the car. I think he was surprised to find that such an independent, feisty American woman could be so scared of such a small creature.

"You are a feminine feminist," he said wisely.

Our friendship continued after I returned home, and I was able to obtain funds for him to visit Eugene. Dr. Binh returned home with new ideas and resources. He built ramps at rural health clinics, allowing easy access to children and adults with mobility limitations.

"Bee and ramps," he would email me, recalling my Vietnam visit.

It made me smile.

Magic moments occur when we least expect them. Is that why we remember them most?

17.

When my mom needed to start using a wheelchair she felt angry and depressed, but checked herself when she realized that her reaction was condemning my life in a wheelchair. As a loud, proud and passionate woman, I told her my chair was a vehicle of independence. Soon we danced in our wheelchairs in the living room.

Loud, proud and passionate

At the United Nations Conference and NGO Forum on Women in Beijing in 1995, I had heard one message loud and clear. There was a burning need for an international disabled women's network, providing leadership training and opportunities to share experiences and skills. Somehow, we needed to create a movement that empowered women with disabilities so that they could enact change in their local communities.

Two years later, after much research and planning, MIUSA launched the Women's Institute on Leadership and Disability (WILD).

Over the next decade, MIUSA would assist many WILD women in a myriad of ways. Obtaining scholarships, enrolling in graduate school, enhancing their careers, becoming involved in political processes, or becoming speakers at national and international conferences: anything was possible.

WILD programs make the world a different place.

Hundreds of women from all over the globe apply for each WILD, but only thirty are selected. Each WILD brings women together from countries as diverse as Cambodia, El Salvador, Fiji, Lesotho, Russia, Syria, and Uzbekistan. There are women who have visual or learning disabilities, Deaf women, wheelchair users, amputees, and women affected by polio or cerebral palsy. Few have boyfriends or husbands because, in their home countries, there is a common view that disabled women are deformed, unfeminine, undesirable, the lowest of the low. They have been rejected by schools, universities, jobs; some have been put into institutions. Many have been raped, verbally and sexually abused. Some have "midnight boyfriends" — men who will only have sex with them when no one will find out. Often, they have been impregnated and abandoned.

I have always found it horrifying to hear these stories as we sit in a circle, passing a candle from one speaker to the next. Yet WILD women are the most insightful, resourceful, beautiful, and optimistic people I have met on my life's journey. For many, WILD programs have provided a first opportunity to be surrounded by other women with disabilities and share their stories, secrets and dreams. They deal with acute poverty, lack of health information, AIDS and other diseases. They live with discrimination, and lack respect from those around them, yet they laugh, sing and dance with abandon.

They epitomize resilience.

I am in awe of them.

On the first morning of a WILD program, my MIUSA colleagues and I meet the visitors to begin a day-long workshop with activities. Thirty eager faces take their places, and we say good morning in over twenty languages. Throughout the day, our translators work hard to present workshop content in English, Spanish, French, Russian or Arabic, as well as American Sign Language and Zambian Sign Language. There is a discussion to ensure that Deaf-blind women understand as well.

We are *Loud, Proud and Passionate*, I tell them. I say this with passion, as if all my years of self discovery are captured in those three words.

Loud.

Proud.

Passionate.

The women embrace the message. They do things they never thought possible. On our challenge course, they climb forty feet into the air. They swing from a rope and walk across a tree limb. Blind, Deaf, quadriplegic—it doesn't matter. We provide adaptive equipment, ropes and helmets, and there is always a team of women to assist and encourage.

"You can do it," we say.

It is challenge by choice. There is no pressure—just a team of loving and admiring sisters urging women to convince themselves of new capabilities.

The challenge course is a metaphor.

Don't let others – or your own preconceived notions of what is possible – define your world. You decide. You set your limits. Or better, no limits. We will support you. We will help you make your dreams come true. You will realize your goals. Trust. Take a chance. We are your safety net.

For three weeks, the women live with homestay families we find for them in Eugene and the surrounding area. The people who host them represent the diversity of our times — single, married, same sex couples, blended families, nuclear families, vegetarians, meat eaters and so on. They don't necessarily know the languages their visitors speak, or anything about their disabilities. They don't have to. They just have to believe that folks from different nations are part of one family, to respect our WILD women, and pack a lunch for them each day. Often, the love that grows makes for relationships that last many years after an exchange is over. Hosts stay in touch with the women as they would their own sisters or daughters.

You don't hear about these stories on the nightly news — but these are stories of the world as it *should* be.

WILD women have gone rafting in cold Oregon rapids. They have filled the green mountains with laughter. They have been to an indoor swimming pool, with warm water and a wheelchair ramp for easy access. Many wear bathing suits for the first time in their lives. The stumps of their amputated limbs, their atrophied or spasmy legs, their crooked arms — all these are suddenly beautiful, no longer hidden and cloaked in shame. They are perfect, just the way they are.

"I'm swimming!"

"I'm floating!"

"I'm really in the water!"

They sit in the hot tub smiling in the warm, bubbling water.

They hug each other every morning as long lost sisters.

WILD women are from the same tribe, united by a shared

determination to reject preconceived notions and create a new model of empowerment.

At WILD, we have run workshops about AIDS, sexuality, birth control. We offer sessions on having children, caring for babies while being blind, carrying babies from a wheelchair, communicating with babies in sign language. WILD provides instruction on self-defense techniques for protection from would-be rapists and abusers. Discussions take place on disability rights and about how to implement laws that will be effective. WILD also provides advice on how to tell the media *our* story, from *our* perspective. The stories we want to tell are about our human rights—not the tragic story of a car accident or a birth defect, or about inspirational heroines who have "overcome" disability.

The women travel to a nearby retreat center for three nights. Some sleep in tents, some in cabins. They wonder if there are lions, tigers or snakes in the bush.

"Well, maybe some bears," we tell them, and their eyes widen with both fear and amusement.

At the retreat center we have more workshops, with guests from international development organizations such as Mercy Corps, Trickle Up and the American Friends Service Committee. These organizations work around the world in the areas of literacy, microfinance, civil society, AIDS prevention, education and health. They come to learn from these women how best to ensure that women with disabilities are included in their programs and services—not only as recipients but as leaders and trainers. Representatives from the Global Fund For Women—which has assisted many women to come to WILD—attend to share information on how WILD women might apply for project grants.

The Fund believes that problems can be solved by grassroots groups, led by women.

"You can write about your project in your own language," its representatives say. "It can be handwritten."

There has always been so much to discuss. But beyond sitting around in circles on the grass, the women talk in bathrooms after their showers and while preparing lunches or clearing the dishes. WILD nights are like a strange and wonderful dream. Campfires blaze as women joyously roast marshmallows on long twigs. Some women make up skits, complete with makeshift costumes. Others sing their traditional songs and perform dances. Eventually, everyone goes inside and it's time for CDs in Arabic, English, Russian and Spanish.

Somehow, sometime, a theme song for the program has come to be adopted. It is a song by Shakira—*Hips Don't Lie*. WILD women have played it over and over again. Togetherness is all of us gyrating in a diversity of movements—hips swerving, shoulders jiggling, arms in the air, canes pivoting and wheelchairs whirling. For many of these women, it is the first time they have felt ready to take on the world. There is beauty, power and inclusion.

Increasingly, disabled women are being recognized, side-by-side with non-disabled colleagues who work on human rights issues all over the world— *Loud, Proud and Passionate*.

WILD became one of MIUSA's signature programs. It is the program I am most proud of and remains closest to my heart.

The genius award

I was in my office at MIUSA when someone told me there was a telephone call for me.

"Take a message," I said. It was a really busy day, and my head was filled with the possibilities and problems of the project I was working on.

"I tried, but they said that you would *really* want to take this call."

That didn't sound good. I immediately thought it was some pushy sales representative wanting to get straight to the CEO and make a pitch for insurance policies or a computer upgrade.

Reluctantly, I picked up the phone.

"Is this Susan?"

"Yes."

"Hello, Susan. I'm calling from the MacArthur Foundation."

I'd heard of the MacArthur Foundation before, usually when radio or television stations announced that an artist, educator or scientist had received an award. MacArthur Fellowships were sometimes called "genius awards", and came with a huge amount of money and no strings attached.

"Do you know any MacArthur Fellows?" The man asked.

"Actually, yes," I replied. "Two."

Ed Roberts, sometimes known as the father of the disability rights movement, was a MacArthur Fellow. So too was Ralf Hotchkiss, a colleague of mine who had figured out a way of building low cost wheelchairs in developing countries, using local materials and the expertise of local people with disabilities.

"In fact, you know three."

I thought for a moment. No—this man was wrong. "People in the news maybe, but I don't personally know of anyone else," I replied.

"Yes, you do," he said, apparently somewhat amused by the conversation.

I was perplexed.

"This is Daniel Socolov from the MacArthur Foundation. I'm calling to tell you that you have been selected as a MacArthur Fellow."

"Is this some sort of joke?" It couldn't possibly be real.

"No, this is very real. You will be getting your letter in the mail."

I'm not sure how the conversation went after that. I was in a state of complete disbelief. There wasn't long to gather myself, though, because about a minute later someone in my office told me there was another call—from ABC News. A camera crew was outside the building, wanting to come up. They'd been waiting for a while and had now been informed that I'd received the official call.

In a couple of minutes I was facing lights and questions, with microphones attached to my shirt. I remember crying with happiness and shock. I also remember thinking of my father, who had now been dead for four years. The most difficult thing was that I was asked not to tell anyone, or talk to any media, until the news story broke on a national evening news show called *Nightline with Ted Koppel*.

I ended up being on the cover of both the Eugene newspaper and the Oregon paper. Tom and I sat with my mom outside her senior living hotel, where she had moved after my dad died. With both papers in front of us, my mom beamed. Her mental state was confused and I'm not sure she understood the magnitude of the honor, but she knew it was something good because my picture was in the paper. We shared breakfast at a nearby restaurant, sitting in the sunlight. It was wonderful.

My friends congratulated me and teased me. They were sure that I was no genius — and I agreed with them. My accomplishments in the disability field, supported by my array of brilliant staff and friends, had brought me recognition in a way I could never have imagined.

Later, when I attended various MacArthur Foundation meetings where Fellows from other years gathered, I was in awe of their accomplishments, from creating state-of-the-art telescopes to choreographing award-winning Broadway productions. There were scientists working on things I couldn't even begin to grasp. Many came from Harvard, Yale or Princeton. They were *real* geniuses, with amazing IQs and incredible CVs, and I was most definitely not in their league.

What I did have was imagination, passion and a lot of *chutzpa*. I'd been able to bring people together to accomplish things that hadn't been done before. Getting a "genius award" when you're a genius is a noteworthy accomplishment. But I had received a "genius award" *without* being a genius.

Perhaps that's an even bigger accomplishment?

Acts of love

My great grandmother hanged herself from the ceiling in Vienna, Austria, sometime in the 1930s. She was ill, and had urged my

grandmother and mother to flee Nazi persecution. Her death was
an act of love. She cared too much to hold them back.

One cold, rainy day in Eugene, Oregon, it occurred to me
that I came from a long line of maternal caregivers.

I remember a time in the San Francisco airport, guiding my
mother's wheelchair into the bathroom and helping her with her
pants. Sideways glances came from other travelers as they watched
me maneuver my own wheelchair to help my mom with hers. I
needed to change her urine-soaked pads, just as she had changed
mine when I went from college athlete to paraplegic at the age of
eighteen. Coordinating two wheelchairs in a small space is no
simple task—but we laughed and giggled and felt triumphant when
we clumsily accomplished it. Bystanders seemed perplexed,
perhaps amazed. Eventually someone offered assistance, joining
our little convoy as we exited.

How ironic that we were both in wheelchairs. My mother
was a world famous ice skater, a European champion. She'd had
power and grace. After my dad's death, she was diagnosed with
Alzheimer's disease. It had cruelly eroded her independence and
left her skating on thin ice, so she moved into the house that Tom
and I shared.

My mother took care of her own mother when she
emigrated to New York after the war. I have vague memories of my
grandmother living with us in our small apartment in Queens, but
she died from cancer when I was five. I remember waving to her
from outside the hospital building, signaling to a tiny figure in a
fourth-floor room. Soon afterward, she disappeared from my world.
My mom had done all she could for her, sharing all she had, to give
her a dignified life. In their own ways, both women were feisty and

strong.

When my mom needed to start using a wheelchair she felt angry and depressed, but checked herself when she realized that her reaction was condemning my life in a wheelchair. I told her my chair was a vehicle of independence. Soon we danced in our wheelchairs in the living room. The diva ice skater mom I had grown up with came alive, flirting with an imaginary audience.

When they called me to tell me that mom could no longer live in the seniors' apartments downtown, I was on my way to welcome Vice President Al Gore as he arrived at the Eugene airport on his election trail for the presidency. They told me she left gas burners on, was easily confused and wet the couch in the lobby. Her dementia was becoming too noticeable, and she could no longer "pass" as someone who could live independently.

"She is a danger to herself and others," they had told me. "You must arrange to get her out of here in the next week."

Al Gore asked me, as a MacArthur Fellow, what it was like to get the "genius award" — but all I could think about was my mother. No nursing homes for her, not after what she endured with the Holocaust. Not after being so strong and loving to me, both before and after my accident. Not my mom.

From that moment on, she lived with us. Tom and I cared for her, and I also organized sweet friends to care for her while I was at work. I tucked her in every night, and she told me what a loving daughter I was. She took no medication, except for some homeopathic remedies given to us by a close friend. Her blue eyes twinkled and she glowed with happiness.

I know it's an unfair question, but I can't help wondering what might happen if all families stayed together, if more people could experience the rewards of sacrifice, and if panic attacks were treated with songs and hugs, not tranquilizers.

Parents are important, and children can be everything to them. Love shapes our destinies. None of my maternal forebears seem to have chosen their paths, but I have a feeling that none regret the journeys they have taken.

Mutual admiration society

Thirty-five years after my accident, Dr. Bolles received a prestigious award for years of humanitarian work.

In Albania and in other places, he had carried out voluntary work for people with spinal injuries. He was the head of neurosurgery in Germany for the United States armed forces, dealing with thousands of war-injured young men and women from Iraq. He often spoke his mind on the horrors of war.

We stayed in touch.

Whenever I asked him if I was his first solo spinal operation as a surgeon, he just laughed. I had no idea what that meant. I also didn't care.

When I called Dr. Bolles to congratulate him on his Neurosurgeon of the Year award, he was touched.

"Oh Susan, this call means so much to me," he said. "I guess you could say we're part of a mutual admiration society — you and me. Someday, we will travel the world together, helping people. We will do our dog and pony show."

Someday, I thought, *we might.*

18.

An image from early childhood came back to me with renewed potency. I saw my grandmother, high above me, at the window of a fourth-floor room where she was dying of cancer. A little earlier she had shared our apartment in Queens, but then she was gone.

On the rocks

Sitting on rocks at the Oregon coast, watching the waves roll in, I wondered if I should inch my body forward and drop into the surf. I imagined myself submerged beneath the cold, swirling waves, quickly losing consciousness, freed from my thoughts and situation.

The scene from the movie *The Hours,* where Nicole Kidman's Virginia Woolf walks suicidal into the river, her skirt filled with heavy rocks, kept coming to mind.

My own nightmare began with a regular mammogram. It took too long developing the film, and when the assistant came back in, she told me they wanted another picture.

Bad sign.

Another wait.

"We'd like to take an ultrasound," the assistant told me when she finally returned.

"When?"

"Right now."

"Why? I want to see the doctor. What's going on?"

Soon, the radiologist appeared. He was a tall man in his fifties, with white hair and a serious face.

"We just want to check something out," he said. He seemed annoyed that I had forced him out of hiding to explain his request, and quickly retreated behind closed doors.

I had entered a bad movie, the set evoking fear and horror. Time slowed down.

The ultrasound was painless, producing a magnification of my left breast on a monitor. I turned my head to see something that looked like a weather report. An incoming storm. Lots of white, rolling clouds.

Suddenly the technician flicked a switch and froze the swirling clouds. Everything on the screen came to a complete halt, and a box was drawn around a small, dark spot.

Cancer, I thought. I was told to come back in a few days for a needle biopsy because of my "low suspicion" mammogram. After the biopsy I went to the coast to await the results. I was filled with dread. I waited four days.

Sitting on the rocks, I decided to call the doctor's office and ask why the nurse hadn't called me.

"The doctor wants to talk to you," she said flatly when I asked for my results.

"Can't *you* tell me?"

"The doctor wants to talk to you," she repeated. It sounded like a line that had been rehearsed for these situations. No matter how the question is phrased, the answer was the same, delivered in the same monotone.

At that moment, I knew my life had changed forever.

Again.

I felt shock, disbelief, terror. The waves beckoned to me. Perhaps, if I'd been able to just stand up and walk over the rocks, I would have done so. I didn't seem able to move at all. I sat, just looking at the ocean, tears welling up in my eyes.

The doctor called back about half an hour later and the news seemed old.

"What happened to the 'low suspicion' you talked about when you did the biopsy?"

"I was surprised at the results," he said quietly. He droned on for a while about statistics, early detections and chances of survival, but his words came to me through some kind of filter that turned them to nonsense.

I wanted to join Virginia Woolf, my head submerged, my hair flowing in the water aimlessly, where all thoughts would disappear.

Forever.

Tripping

I admit it. I once took LSD. I was in high school when some friends offered me a little, and afterwards we went for a walk in a nearby park.

The sky was so blue, the sunset so lavender.

I noticed every leaf on every tree, every sparkle on the river.

Maybe that's what a cancer diagnosis does to you.

Suddenly, chocolate gained an extra intensity of flavor. I seemed to see things I had never seen before. I had always appreciated every moment, but my senses seemed sharper and my feelings deeper.

I was in an altered state.

I chuckled inside when I heard people express worry about the smallest of things. Their pettiness amused me, and I wanted to tell them what I had learned.

Love life. Seize its magnificence. Treasure each day.

More than just coincidence

Why have so many good things, moments and events in my life collided or been woven through with such awful, sad, and tragic things?

It can't be just coincidence. Or maybe it can.

I recall a cousin's marriage in New York where, in the middle of an extravagant wedding, my uncle fell to the floor. Uncle Oscar had been joyously doing the *hora* dance with his son and new daughter-in-law, and I was about to go on to the dance floor and join the festivities. Many doctors were present as guests, and they tried desperately to revive him. I remember the bride running toward the ambulance with the long white train of her elegantly laced bridal gown sweeping the floor. Three hundred or more guests were left gasping in disbelief, and stood frozen in their places. I remember hearing a young waitress turn to someone more senior and ask, "Do we serve the soup now anyway?" I don't remember the answer.

Uncle Oscar was pronounced dead on arrival at the hospital.

The following day, all the guests from the wedding attended his funeral. My father had been very close to my uncle as they had lived in the same *shtetl* (village) in Podvalychyska, Poland.

"You know, Susan," my dad said, grabbing my hand as we walked toward the synagogue, "this is a sad and terrible thing for everyone. But actually I'm happy for Oscar. His last moment was so happy. He was dancing with his son and his son's bride, in the company of all his relatives and friends. He didn't suffer. He wasn't in a hospital, sick with tubes hanging from him. He was perhaps experiencing one of the best moments in his life, and then he was gone. Good for Oscar! That's how I would like to go."

When the very good and very bad happen within moments of each other, what sense do we make of it? What sense do I make of it?

In 1971, I was eighteen, excited about starting my life as a freshman at the University of Colorado. Everything was perfect. And then, in the flash of a terrible accident, everything was different.

By 1982, I had adjusted to being a paraplegic and was excelling in wheelchair sports. I had just started living with my boyfriend and everything was once again perfect. I felt a tingling feeling in the right side of my face and down my arm. It turned out to be a liquid cyst in my spinal cord which, after an operation and two years of painful recovery, forced me to give up all the sports I loved, which were so much part of who I was. Why? Why *again*?

In 1995, my work with MIUSA was recognized nationally, and I was thrilled to be invited to the White House to receive an award from President Bill Clinton. The night before I was scheduled to leave with my parents for Washington DC, my father was rushed to the hospital with a heart attack. He died within two weeks.

In 2000, after I received the MacArthur Award, I was going to the airport to meet Vice President Gore when I received a distressing call on my cell phone. It had come from the retirement hotel my mom had been living in for the past year.

"Your mother can't stay with us any longer," they had told me.

Once again my life was changed forever. The best and the worst of moments collided again.

For close to seven years, I didn't leave my mom for even for one night. I no longer traveled for work, even though I was regularly being invited to speak and give workshops around the world. Then, in 2006, I decided it was time to travel again. My mom's seizures seemed less frequent and she seemed comfortable with the people we hired to take care of her during the day. She really loved them, and Tom was there at night.

I booked a trip to Chicago to attend a gathering of recipients of the MacArthur Award. I also went to Halifax, Nova Scotia, to an international microcredit conference where the winner of the Nobel Peace Prize was speaking about empowering the poorest women of the world to become economically independent by obtaining small business loans.

Yes, I was back to doing something I loved — traveling. Meeting strangers in airports who shared their life stories… staying in hotels with clean sparkling bathrooms and fragrant soaps… looking out airplane windows seeing the sun set below a carpet of puffy, billowing clouds.

It should have been blissful. I had waited a long time. But how much fun can traveling be when you have just been diagnosed with breast cancer?

You can fly far away. Perhaps you can even forget about the cancer for a few fleeting moments — but fleeting those moments are. The diagnosis weighs on you like a giant boulder. It crushes your peace of mind.

Why again? Why the good and the bad?

The high window

An image from early childhood came back to me with renewed potency. I saw my grandmother, high above me, at the window of a fourth-floor room where she was dying of cancer. A little earlier she had shared our apartment in Queens, but then she was gone.

A geneticist advised me to be tested for a gene carried by many Ashkenazic Jews which increases the risk of both breast and ovarian cancer. Momentarily, I stopped breathing. I was a child again, standing on the sidewalk, waving at a small woman in a window.

Perhaps, I thought, the story of my maternal lineage was about to be linked in more ways than I could possibly have imagined.

My grandmother — and now me.

Eventually, I summoned the courage to take a genetic test.

I wasn't a carrier.

Even so, I found myself wanting to make sense of my cancer in terms of my family's stories of love, lineage and destiny.

Death risks

It was a mental hell. I seemed capable of nothing except crying and praying, so I cried and cried, and hoped for an earthquake or tsunami to swallow me whole. Natural disasters were a long time coming, so I cried and prayed some more.

Being diagnosed with breast cancer left me shocked and depressed. I was in no condition to make decisions about anything, yet I faced a myriad of decisions that could save or end my life.

First, there was a decision about surgery. Mastectomy, or lumpectomy? A mastectomy meant no radiation. A lumpectomy meant less surgery. From what I could research my survival statistics were the same, so I went for the lumpectomy. Surely, I thought, radiation wouldn't be so bad?

Next, which surgeon? Everyone seemed to recommend someone different. I decided on a young woman, who had been requested to see me by another doctor I knew. I was told she was brilliant—but, just as importantly given my state of mind, she was optimistic and made me smile. She knew about my life before I even opened my mouth and said she would speak to my neurosurgeon, Dr. Gene Bolles, before she operated. Somehow, that comforted me.

Without doubt, the most difficult decision I needed to make was about chemotherapy. All the oncologists told me that I needed it, including a big shot oncologist in Portland, while other kinds of doctors said it was up to me. Chemotherapy would improve my chances by just ten per cent overall, and Gene said that he would support my decision not to have it. My friend Emily took notes at every meeting with every doctor, and was brave enough to talk it all through with me. But, no question, it was me who had to make the decision. I was in "decision hell" for several weeks. I read everything that I could on the Internet, and all the books at the bookstore.

Those were the worst weeks of my life.

Eventually I flew to Mayo Clinic, in Arizona, reputed to be the best cancer clinic in the world. Deep down inside, I knew the oncologist there would tell me the same thing as every other oncologist. It was just another step I needed to take.

My friend Meira lived in Tucson and met me for my appointment. The consultation was solemn, with talk of metastases and slow death if the cancer spread to the lungs, bones, brain, pancreas...

It was awful.

Afterwards, Meira and I took a nearby nature trail to debrief. It was hot and dry in the desert sun. The area looked like the fake background of an old western movie, with branching cacti all around. As we reviewed the doctor's pessimistic prognosis, Meira's gaze suddenly froze.

"Susan, don't move," she said. "Don't scream. Stay very still."

"What is it?" I asked, dreading her answer.

"There is a rattlesnake a few feet behind your wheelchair. Don't make any sudden moves."

There are few things that terrify me more than snakes. Any snake, even the most harmless, can take my breath away in an instant. Little by little I turned my head, and saw the specimen that Meira was talking about. It was huge. There was a massive coil and it had raised its head, pointing at us with its flickering tongue and intermittently lunging forward, as if by way of warning.

Somehow, I was able to tell Meira that I would move slowly away from the snake. I cautiously put my hands on my wheels and started forward at a snail's pace along the path, looking for an exit toward the road. Meira followed.

I pushed faster and faster, scanning the path desperately to be sure I didn't run over another rattlesnake.

When we arrived safely in our hotel about ten minutes later, we laughed in disbelief. For me, the irony was inescapable.

What does it mean to have a rattlesnake appear when you are discussing risk, death, life and fate? The Mayo oncologist had said that he thought I was relatively healthy, which meant that there was more time for the cancer to come back. What kind of mixed message is that? Not to worry, I thought, I'll reduce my chances of the cancer coming back by engaging in high risk activities.

Straight after returning home, still undecided about chemotherapy, I bought a huge Honda Goldwing 1500 motorcycle. It was a "trike", and I had hand controls installed so that I could ride it.

Life has its risks, I thought. *I want to choose mine.*

A decision

I followed my heart and my gut.

No chemo. Not for me. I've never done well with drugs, I can't stand nausea and I was already severely anemic. I was also concerned about my syringomyelia—the cyst in my spinal cord. What if it became worse? I knew that chemotherapy could affect motor neurons and, having already lost muscle function twice in my life, I wanted to continue to be able to ride my bike and push my chair.

"The chemo effects will only be temporary," said the oncologists, almost like a mantra. "You don't have to worry about that."

"Right," I would reply. "How many people with spinal cord injury have you given chemo to?"

"Well, none personally," they all replied. "But the statistics show that..."

"How do you know it won't affect the syringomyelia?"

"Oh, it won't."

"Do you have research on that?"

"No, but..."

Just as I suspected, I'd think. *So how can you know?*

I decided that if I got worse from chemotherapy, not even knowing that it would prevent my cancer from returning, I would regret it. And if my cancer returned, I would submit to chemo then, never knowing whether it might have helped earlier.

I am not advocating this position—who knows whether it was the right one? With life and death, who can *ever* know?

Survivors

"I am a survivor," my mom would always say.

She lived in England during World War II and volunteered to put out fires on the roofs of London during the Blitz. She never slept in underground bunkers to be safe from German air raids. She slept in her bed. My mother told me that if you heard the bombs explode, you knew you were still alive.

My dad seemed fearless too. He took part in the Allied invasion of Normandy on 6 June 1944, known as D-Day. He spent time during the war on merchant marine ships carrying ammunition to the Allies.

Secret missions.

Dangerous missions.

Years later, we would watch documentaries about these missions. One in three ships was torpedoed by submarines and lost.

One in three.

He survived. His chances were a little over 66%.

I couldn't help thinking about this when I was told that I had a 70% of surviving without taking chemotherapy for my cancer. I was hoping that "survival" is hereditary.

The will to live — to survive. Can there be a gene for that?

I love you, *poipee*

When I began taking care of my mom, I never imagined that she might outlive me. Her eventual death once terrified me, but scared me less when I was facing my own.

A gerontologist once gave her three years to live — if she was lucky. Long after that time was up, we were still dancing around the living room in our wheelchairs. I danced with vigor to my favorite songs of the 1960s and 1970s, and my mom's eyes would light up. We held hands — hers delicate, almost exquisite with age. She would delight in my movements, my hips gyrating in my wheelchair, my arms flying around in rhythmic abandon.

Perhaps she remembered her performances on figure skates, gliding effortlessly around the ice in beautiful costumes before hundreds of admirers.

Perhaps, in her mind, she was again performing her spectacular leaps and spins in pre-Olympic competition. She had been only sixteen when war broke out and had no idea what horrors lay ahead.

Perhaps.

As the years passed, Alzheimer's disease had advanced and our dances had changed. Once my mom might have said, "Very good Susan—I'm having so much fun!" Now, she rarely spoke. One night she stopped dancing and put her hands to her chest. She looked at me sadly, suddenly out of breath.

She began to have difficulty swallowing, and ate less and less. Her slim body became more and more frail. Still, though, her skin remained soft, and she could be radiant. Whenever she smiled, I was taken aback by her beauty and spirit.

Sometimes, burdened by an overload of cancer information—side effects of treatment, mortality statistics, quality of life considerations—I would go into my mom's quaint wood cabin behind our house. Quiet and serene, it allowed a view of giant cedar trees, rising up like ancient cathedrals outside. Squirrels ran up and down their trunks, playing tag, gathering nuts. Birds sang. It seemed like Neverland.

I would lie down next to my mommy. I loved the way she smelled, the feel of her velvety skin. She caressed my hands, my hair.

The less she spoke, the more her words meant to me. She would break the silence and whisper an old Viennese term of endearment I'd heard all my life: "I love you, *poipee*." Sometimes she would say, "You are wonderful, sweetie pie."

I would close my eyes and hold her.

How many daughters get to hold and be held daily by their mother? I have experienced a lifetime of unconditional love. I had always been so proud of my mom, and she was proud of me. There are no words to explain the depth of feeling during those quiet moments in the cabin.

All the while, our wheelchairs stood beside each other like two friendly horses, tethered to a rail while their riders refreshed themselves with a cool drink inside the Lucky Saloon.

19.

As I came toward the end of my therapy, I began to plan my radiation emancipation party. I wanted it to occur a few minutes after my last treatment, at a nearby restaurant. The caterer was a bit perplexed to hear that the theme of the party would be boobs — hearing the words cancer and party in the same sentence was a lot for her to take in.

Death therapy

While I was at the Manhattan rehab center in 1971, Bill had changed my thinking forever. I had come to think of Bill's philosophy as a kind of "death therapy". He had gone from sculptor to high-level quadriplegic and identified the moment of transition as a kind of death. It had enabled him to face his new life without despair. To begin again, you need to let go.

The idea that one life can end, to be replaced by another, had equipped me to face great changes in my life. It had enabled me to let go of one Susan Sygall and embrace the next.

No regrets.

It had helped me embrace life as a paraplegic. Later, when a cyst in my spinal cord forced me to give up all the wheelchair sports I loved, death therapy again came to the rescue. The new Susan found other things to enjoy, like horse riding and painting.

The doctor wants to talk to you.

When those words came over the phone, I knew that I would need to call upon death therapy once more. The life I had known was over.

Gone.

Cancer would now be part of my identity. Waking up in the morning without some consciousness of cancer would no longer be possible.

Remember those rocks? I asked myself. *Those rocks on the Oregon coast and those icy waters that were beckoning to you? Imagine you did that. You are dead.*

Dead.

Maybe someone hit your bike with their car while talking on their cell phone.

Or your plane crashed.

Or you were shot by a burglar in some crazed moment of panic.

Whatever. The cause of my death was irrelevant. What mattered was that a life had ended, and it was time to embrace a new one.

Biking to radiation

Biking to radiation, past herons perched on logs in the middle of the river, gave me a chance to breathe. I liked being alone, in nature, and thought I might be able to make sense of it all.

I couldn't.

But still, my radiation oncologist thought it was amazing.

"No one cycles to radiation—let alone a paraplegic with a wheelchair in tow!"

The people working at the cancer radiation center were kind, but putting on the white gown for every treatment made me feel a bit like a prisoner. Uniform on, uniform off. Every day, Monday through Friday, for thirty-four treatments. That was my sentence. I got to leave each day, but needed to check in again the following day. Released on parole. As much as I didn't want to go back, the consequences of *not* going back were far too drastic.

In the waiting room, there were conversations with other gowned prisoners.

"What are you in for? Larceny, grand theft, prostate, lung or breast cancer?"

"How much time have you served? Two weeks? Three months?"

"Five treatments—I'm half way through."

"I've just started."

"I'm almost done."

"How are you doing?"

"I hate being locked up. It's lonely. Fatigue, skin burn, pain, swelling…"

Those just starting always wanted to know what to expect, even though no two experiences of radiation are the same. The ones who were back after being cleared previously seemed the saddest. Returned prisoners. They had hoped they were finished. They had survived both cancer and radiation. *Never again*, they thought. Unfortunately there is high recidivism with both cancer and criminals.

One woman told me that she knew she would eventually

come back. She had cancer in both breasts. She was filled with grace and composure.

I wanted to believe that when I left the radiation center after thirty-four treatments I would really be done forever, but I'd met too many "returnees" not to know that nothing can be taken for granted. "Expect the worst, hope for the best." Dr. Bolle's words after my car accident at the age of eighteen seemed to have new relevance.

As I came toward the end of my therapy, I began to plan a radiation emancipation party. I wanted it to occur a few minutes after my last treatment, at a nearby restaurant. The caterer was a bit perplexed to hear that the theme of the party would be boobs— hearing the words *cancer* and *party* in the same sentence was a lot for her to take in. I imagined her thinking that she was glad it wasn't her. I wished it wasn't me, too. But it was, so I was determined to have fun with it. Like a song I heard on the radio said, *I'm going to live forever – today.*

"Be irreverent and funny, but not pornographic," I joked, trying to ease the moment.

She smiled. She said it would be fun for the pastry chef to experiment.

I printed some invitations which said that, for the safety of guests, sunglasses were mandatory. By my thirty-fourth treatment, I was sure I'd be radioactive!

End of a nightmare

On March 8, 2007, I went to the radiation room for the last time.

When the humming from the radiation machine stopped I followed the drill, lying in my gown facing the ceiling. A few moments passed before the radiation technicians came in to move the machine that hovered over me, and to remove the lead eye-protectors.

The silence was eerie. It was over.

There would be many check-ups, tests, scary moments, and who knows what else. But this part was over. My left breast—swollen and sore—could take a well-earned break. It had been regularly marked up with blue ink to show radiation points, but could now retreat under cover, never to reappear in this manner again. The scent of burning human cells is sickening—even more so when it comes from your own body. Layers of damaged skin were sloughing off my breast. It was not a pleasant feeling.

But the knowledge that my radiation treatments had finished made tears flow down my cheeks. Time seemed to stand still.

The technicians returned and I left the room for the thirty-fourth time after almost two months of daily treatments.

I had brought treats for everyone—the doctors, the nurses, the radiation technicians, and the patients and family members waiting silently in the waiting room.

"I'm finished," I told the people who were waiting. "I've graduated."

Quiet, serious faces turned to indulgent smiles.

"Would you like a cupcake or cream puff shaped like a boob to help me celebrate?" I sounded giddy—even to myself.

People become curious and peeked into the pastry box to decide whether to go for a cream puff or cupcake. Laughter broke out as they realized that the treats really *were* in the shape of breasts.

"How wonderful", one woman said. "Congratulations."

"I have five more treatments," said another.

"My daughter has twelve more."

I said my goodbyes and thanked all the staff. With their jokes, their laughter and their hugs, they had made the unbearable bearable. Sometimes I had burst out crying when the pain of raw skin got too intense and the whole damn nightmare seemed just too awful.

As I left the building, the world seemed reassuringly normal. It was just another day. Someone was smoking a cigarette in front of the building, talking on the cell phone. People were mailing letters, cars were whizzing by.

When I reached home, I felt nothing but exhaustion. There's a weird rush immediately following treatment, but a few hours later you just need to lie down. Radiation treatments are cumulative — and as the recipient of thirty-four treatments my need to lie down was overpowering. It was 3.00 p.m. I could lie down for an hour, but would then need to summon the energy to get up. I had a party to go to!

My party.

My "radiation emancipation party".

We were expecting more than fifty-five people. As a disability activist, I have always taught others from around the world that it is important to celebrate your victories, big and small. Otherwise, you burn out.

Yes, burn out. The words were fitting.

For me, the party was a marker, a kind of ritual that would help me move on to the next phase. I had been excited about it.

I slept for an hour, got up and dressed for the party. Later, people would say how good I looked.

It was the radiation glow.

Radiation emancipation party

Everyone was wearing sunglasses, and the restaurant had outdone my wildest expectations. The caterer had embraced the theme and made it joyous. One look at the menu and people were able to connect with the spirit of the occasion:

MENU

Smoked salmon mousse with crème fraîche nipples

Herbed goat cheese breasts
Smoked duck breast on brioche with apple chutney
Olive tapenade crostini with goat cheese

Coconut macaroons with chocolate nipples
Petite cream puffs
Mini chocolate cupcakes with buttercream and brandied cherry

All my friends were there. Some had left presents by my front door after each of the thirty-four radiation treatments: flowers, books, plants, toys, magic wands, chocolate and puzzles. My rabbi was there too, as well as my work colleagues who had so willingly covered for me when I could only work part-time.

The Mayor of Eugene was also there. I knew her from my work, and one day I'd met her on the street. When she asked how I was doing, I had burst into tears and told her about my diagnosis. She hugged me for a long time, and told me she would support me any way she could. It was wonderful that she now wanted to celebrate with me.

Many of those who had been directly involved in my cancer journey were there, too—also wearing sunglasses. It was a very special feeling to see them all, with champagne in hand. The first to arrive was my oncologist, whose role it had been to encourage me to take chemotherapy. He had his picture taken with me, and I remember thinking as we smiled into the lens that, at the end of the day, we're all on one team. My rehab doctor also came to the party. She had helped me choose my surgeon, and supported me in my decision to gamble against the statistics and go without the chemo—a decision I would need to live with, for better or worse, for the rest of my life.

My radiation oncologist came along, too. A beautiful and vibrant young woman, she had chatted about her husband and made me feel like an old friend. The radiation nurse, who had laughed at all my jokes and answered a million questions about my peeling skin and shooting pains in my breast, came along, and I was also thrilled to see the guy who sat at the cancer center's reception. He had made me laugh the first time I entered the building—quite an amazing feat for that moment in time.

One team. I hope it can save me—but no matter what, I'll always be glad that these people were on my journey, and prepared to celebrate its milestones.

A radiation party? It was unusual, and we all knew it. It

went on for hours, and everyone had a great time. I made a short speech, and found myself getting a bit tearful — who wouldn't? There was so much love in the room. It filled the room like cream in the cream puffs — thick, sweet and mushy.

Eventually people said their goodbyes. The oncologist, with his crisp, blue shirt and a cell phone strapped to his belt, was the last to leave. He hugged me, and when I got home I found an email from him:

> *"Thank you for inviting me to your radiation emancipation party. It is so important for people to celebrate these things. No one has ever done anything like this. Over the next few months I am going to try to do something so all the patients can have a form of celebration. It's so important. Thank you."*

I don't believe bad things happen for a reason — I think bad things just happen. And they happen to lots of people, all the time, all over the world.

Our challenge, our quest, is to face the worst of times and take something positive out of them.

Maybe, I did. The party gave me joy, and it gave other people joy, too. I like to believe that other women might hear about it, and experience a sense of victory and joy in having similar parties.

Patient?

A year after my surgery for breast cancer, I was invited to join an advisory board, working with groups of doctors to improve cancer treatment in the Eugene area. I guess they thought anyone who can think of having a radiation party must have some other good ideas.

"Will you be a patient representative?" I was asked.

"I'm not a patient any more—and I'm not very patient," I replied defiantly. I knew, however, that I had joined millions of other brave souls with cancer on a journey they never asked for, and after a friendly conversation I agreed.

Sometimes I think that if a doctor ever says I need more surgery, radiation, or chemotherapy—or, God forbid, all three—I will hop on my Honda Goldwing and go for a long cross country trip with no fear of getting killed.

I heard that Lynn Redgrave described it best. "I may die on a motorcycle or bicycle or in a plane crash. But I will not die of breast cancer."

Enough said.

Perhaps, though, no less bravely, I will surround myself with friends and plunge back into the painful, heartbreaking swirl of medical intervention and remember Bill's famous words:

That life is over. This life is here. They are separate.

20.

You never know when a casual conversation can change someone's life. My conversation with Phillip was perhaps one of the many conversations that contributed to the worldwide development of disability pride. Proud to be disabled? Is that possible? You bet!

Crip think

When I had eventually tracked down Bill after rehab, he remembered nothing of the conversation that had helped me embrace a new life. Not many years ago, I discovered that some of my own words had equally affected a young man named Phillip. And, just like Bill, I hadn't even noticed.

When Phillip told me that I'd changed his life, I had no idea what he was talking about. By then, he was in his thirties. A disability activist and artist, he was part of an informal network of people working on disability rights issues and had just come back from Germany, where he'd been doing consulting work on independent living centers and sexuality for disabled people.

Phillip had a pleasant smile and joyous eyes. Short, thin arms hung by his sides, with each hand having only a few unusually formed fingers. He'd been born with a physical disability that gave him the kind of look that, not so long ago, would almost certainly have made parents pull their children away — as if he was contagious. Nowadays, at least, the stares he got were discreet, and only an inquisitive child would make a comment.

"What's wrong with that man's arms, Mommy?" A child might ask.

"Oh, he has some sort of disability — but that makes him unique," an enlightened mother might respond.

Times have changed — and things had changed in the way Phillip viewed himself, too.

"It was something you said years ago," he told me. "It turned the lights on for me."

I tried to think of what life-changing words I might have said, and wondered how they could have affected this gifted man, now a well-known consultant in his own right.

Phillip just smiled at me and left me wondering. Soon afterward, I heard that he was not only telling audiences the story of the woman who changed his life, but *also* explaining that she didn't recall that watershed conversation.

"It doesn't matter," he would say, laughing at the irony of it all. "It's the message that counts."

This made me all the more curious. When I saw him next, I told him I really, *really* wanted to know what I'd said.

Years earlier, he told me, we had spoken to each other at a gathering connected with disability politics. The conversation was of the kind that only two disabled people can have, speaking as members of a unique family that binds people of diverse backgrounds together through a set of shared experiences. At some point during the conversation I told Phillip that I hated it when people said, "Oh Susan, you're so incredible. I don't even think of you as disabled."

Phillip had asked: "So what do you say then?"

"Well, what do you think I say?"

According to Phillip, he had been perplexed by this question, and was glad when I continued in a very matter-of-fact manner. I said to him what I had said to so many others.

"I say that *of course* I am disabled. I ask these people why I would have to be *un*disabled to be incredible, competent or happy. I ask why they think that telling me that I don't seem disabled is a compliment. Is being disabled synonymous with mediocrity, incompetence, unhappiness?"

Phillip had been wide-eyed.

"Being disabled," I had told him, "is part of who I am — like having blue eyes, being Jewish, being a woman, being a Gemini, and liking chocolate. I'm not trying to be non-disabled, because to me being disabled doesn't have a negative meaning. It's more of a political term, a description for ourselves and others. If people want to compliment me, they can compliment me. 'You are a great executive director... You started a great organization...' Whatever! But being 'like a non-disabled person' *isn't* a compliment. 'I am disabled', I tell people — 'take a look! I am proud of who I am, of our history, our achievements and so forth. But don't expect me to be non-disabled just because, in your mind, that's the biggest compliment you can give.'"

For Phillip, this was mind-boggling. As a person born with a disability, he had always thought that being "like a non-disabled person" was the only way to be. It was something to strive for, and he'd felt real pressure to pass himself off in that world. Passing as a non-disabled person had been, in his mind, the greatest compliment a disabled person could get. Phillip had internalized discrimination to such an extent that he believed he should never consider himself disabled. If that was a victory, what was the price? It made it necessary to deny and negate an integral part of his identity. What inner turmoil that can cause! The task of reconciling who we really *are* with an image of how others think we *ought to be* is enormous, and it can only be painful.

At one time, we all seem to have bought into the story that disability is inherently bad — an unadulterated negative. In truth, the real horror of being disabled is *not* the short arms, the unusual fingers, the paralyzed legs, the slurred speech. It's misconception, discrimination and lack of opportunity.

Not being able to go to regular schools or get into a bathroom.

Being denied a job.

Not being expected to find a lover and make friends.

Etcetera.

I hadn't thought about that conversation with Phillip from the moment it ended until the time he reminded me of it, but I was glad it had helped him to feel whole, and to embrace everything he was born to be. I was also glad that, through Phillip, my words, and the words of other disability activists, were being repeated around the world, in different forms and in diverse cultural contexts.

You never know when a casual conversation can change someone's life. That conversation with Phillip was perhaps one of the many conversations that contributed to the worldwide development of disability pride.

Proud to be disabled?

Is that possible?

You bet!

Everyday journeys

For a long time, my work with Mobility International USA (MIUSA) involved traveling every few weeks, going to meetings, setting up programs in other countries such as Bulgaria or Vietnam, attending conferences in Europe or South America. When my Mom needed my care, things had changed. I couldn't travel knowing she might be having a seizure, feeling pain, or worse. Later, cancer treatments increased my sense of confinement and, with it, my sense of loss.

People I knew would stop me in the street and ask me what countries I had just returned from.

"Not traveling much," I would reply. Often, these people had no idea what was really going on in my life. Sometimes, when I met someone I knew quite well, I'd offer the same simple answer but then break down crying. A few awkward moments would follow, and I'd reveal the truth. We would hug each other before continuing on our separate paths.

Everyday moments became my journeys. I rode my bike by the river, watching the seasons change, the leaves turn crimson. I gazed at the river's rapids, the never-ending chant of the water my Zen-like mantra. I noticed small things—the movement of clouds, the song of birds, the dance of a butterfly on the breeze.

I felt deep appreciation for the beauty and friendliness of my community in Eugene. I gathered with friends on the Jewish holidays, and lit candles on Friday nights to welcome the *Shabbat* or

Sabbath. I brought my mom to the table for the blessing of the bread and wine before Tom and I recited ancient prayers in Hebrew. Friends came by, some of them professional musicians with their instruments. We would drink wine, eat fabulous food potluck style, and sing songs late into the night. Sometimes with friends we played "speed scrabble", an adaptation of the board game played without a board at a super fast pace. There were no real rules and the ones we made up could be changed for each round, with the emphasis being on creativity, silliness and whatever kept us laughing.

This, I realized, was a fairytale life.

Who would have thought I'd ever own a horse? As a child in New York, that possibility would probably have seemed remote, but after my cancer treatment I bought a chestnut quarter horse named Stetson. He had been trained to listen to verbal cues as opposed to leg commands, and Tom built a mounting structure at the local stables so that I could get on. My friend Evelyn, who had traveled to China with me, became my riding partner, saddling the horse and doing all the maneuvering I wasn't able to do. I rode with a Western saddle, allowing me to hold the saddle horn firmly while attempting to find my balance point as Stetson trotted in large circles. On good days, when both Stetson and I were feeling calm and connected, I could ride him with a bareback saddle at a walk, and sometimes at a slow trot with Evelyn close by.

After riding, I loved brushing Stetson's thick hair and the smell of hay and horse lingering in my clothes. I would kiss Stetson's velvety nose and blow a puff of air into his nostrils, which he seemed to enjoy. Riding can relax my whole body, and it brings a sense of accomplishment: *I have done something I both love and fear.*

Perhaps the greatest freedom offered by riding is that all other thoughts must vanish from my mind. For me, it is a form of meditation, requiring complete presence in the moment. Although the stables are only fifteen minutes from my home, they occupy an open rural area with mountains in full view and sweeping Oregon skies. This became my foreign country. For a time, I could be transported.

When the weather turned and it was gray and rainy, I traveled with Tom and my mom to the cozy resort of home. We could huddle by the woodstove or soak up the warmth of our living room. With the radio tuned to a classical music station, my mom would sit beside me, beautiful in her bright pink turtleneck, her cheeks glowing, her thick silvery hair in a pony tail and braid. Holding a few pages from a magazine I gave her to look at, her hands rose and fell with the music of Bach, Beethoven or Mozart, and you could almost mistake her for Leonard Bernstein conducting an orchestra. Sometimes, she would look up at me and nod, her face lit by a smile.

No words.

We needed no words. I'd blow her a kiss, and she would do the same for me. She would stare at the magazine pages for hours, arranging and rearranging them, dipping in and out of many worlds. We had what so many people yearned their whole lives to feel—perfect love, an acceptance of how things are, and the joy of making the best of difficult situations.

My growing family

At the offices of Mobility International USA (MIUSA), there are picture collages showing images of all the programs we've conducted, going back more than a quarter of a century. People with disabilities as well as professional and non-disabled advocates from over one hundred countries have formed a powerful family of alumni. Over two thousand people in that family are making changes in their communities, passing disability rights legislation, forming disabled women's groups, speaking at conferences, fighting for their rights. Our exchange groups have become larger and more diverse, with delegates representing Africa, Asia, the Americas, Eastern and Western Europe, Australia, New Zealand, Micronesia and the Middle East. I hear from them via emails and we track their progress through our alumni network. They are part of MIUSA — a family within the family of people with disabilities, the global family I first recognized as I exchanged glances with that boy sitting in the dirt in Thailand.

We have developed publications on how disabled people must be included in educational exchanges and in international development, and on subjects from education, employment and health care to transportation, legislation and gender equality. MIUSA is a "cross disability" organization, and provides advocacy for people who have physical, sensory, developmental, psychiatric or non-apparent disabilities.

After my cancer diagnosis I worked as much as possible and soon returned full-time with a flexible schedule. Mornings were a time for creamy hot chocolates before I rushed to my office in downtown Eugene. Being at work made me happy. As always I thrived on the decision making, the programming, the excitement of a group arriving from another country. With stimulating meetings, ambitious goal setting and team challenges, I knew I was blessed to be the leader of an innovative organization. I was surrounded by a staff that I loved, a dedicated and fun-loving group who would never stop believing that almost anything can happen if we work for it. "We are only limited by our dreams and imagination, and there is no shortage of dreams at MIUSA," I wrote in our 25th anniversary report.

When I needed to calm myself—to find the deep quiet within—I would think of what I had accomplished, the places I had been, and the people I had affected. I couldn't imagine more rewarding work or a more exciting life. I continued to be inspired by people I met. Through the Women's Institute on Leadership and Disability (WILD), I had met extraordinary women doing extraordinary things. I had found strength in their strength, resilience in their resilience.

I had seen life as it should be – *Loud, Proud and Passionate*.

Fear

I am not so very brave. There are days when fear lurks everywhere. It's there in the sky, in my mind, on the grass, at the bottom of a coffee cup. I try not to look at it but I know it's there. I can go about my day's business, but every once in a while I catch it winking at me, just to let me know it's still around.

I've had days riding Stetson when—despite the hundreds of times I have felt so confident and secure in the saddle—every move is frightening, and every sideways glance makes me shudder. I've had visions of a mad gallop into a fence, being violently bucked off, being trampled. Invariably, the horse senses my uneasiness and becomes nervous too. The fear comes between us.

I have woken because fear has shaken me out of bed. I have fallen thousands of feet down huge crevices in the earth, past layers of dirt and rock until there is nowhere else to fall. When I open my eyes and find that I am still in bed, there is dread in my heart and fear in my veins.

I have wanted to escape, but know that there is nowhere to go but the bathroom to brush my teeth and start a new day.

Yet there are days of hope and faith, too. There are days when I've imagined that everything will be okay, that I am cancer-free forever and have a lifetime of possibilities.

The nightmare is over. I will have time. I will connect with more people, not only people with disabilities and their families, but folks with cancer too. I will tell my story, accomplish more of my goals, travel again, visit the friends I have made throughout the world. I will swim in clear blue waters and embrace all that has happened to me.

Those imaginings are not bravery. They are not "facing the fear". To truly look into the face of fear, you need to see all that could possibly happen and still not look away. To face your fears is to imagine worst case scenarios and know that, somehow, you'll still be okay.

You find a tranquil island in the middle of the tumultuous ocean. You sit with the fear and it doesn't overwhelm you. Something emerges from deep within you and envelops the fear. You cage the fear and do what you have to do, say what needs to be said.

You can do this.

You pick up the telephone, schedule your next mammogram or your appointment with an oncologist. You arrange for your surgery or break down some other personal barrier.

And then you quickly do something else in case fear, like Houdini, escapes from its cage.

Healing the world

My faith in Judaism remained constant over the years, though I continued to wrestle with the question of why there is so much pain, suffering and injustice in the world. My faith, I believe, never taught that joy and suffering must be connected. An understanding of the transitory nature of life is all we need to know of its preciousness.

If I had just one wish for myself, it would be to live long enough—and feel well enough—to do more *tikkun olam* (healing the world).

I hope I can.

If I can't, I will remain proud of the progress I have made—with the support of many others—in changing the lives of people with disabilities.

I will remember the love of friends who supported me through the good and bad times.

I will remember my parents who gave me the confidence and the sense of wonder needed to love life, whatever it brings.

One of my father's favorite blessings was *Gam ze l'tova* — "May all that happens be for the best." As a lifelong activist, I built on that philosophy, with a focus on making the world a better place. Some of the blessings I choose to recite are:

- *May the concept of disability rights be embraced by all, so that the possibility it holds to change the world is realized.*
- *May we each be proud of all that we are, encouraging children and adults to reach for dreams in an environment that is free of expectation about what they can and cannot do.*
- *May "I don't have to go through this alone" be the battle cry of all those dealing with issues of health or discrimination, and may it be heard.*
- *May we have the wisdom to understand that when one life ends — through the onset of disability, cancer, divorce, the loss of a loved one, or any other unexpected change — we have the choice of letting go gracefully, finding new meaning in the gift of another life.*
- *Whenever possible, may we laugh and celebrate.*

Someday

It was my Dad's *yartziet*, the anniversary of his death. A difficult day. Swathed in memories of him, I built bridges from my past to my future. I went to a café, drank hot chocolate, ate a cookie. I imagined my daddy next to me, with his cup of "java" and his funny, insightful conversation. My eyes filled with tears for what I had lost. For a moment, I could feel his strong arms around me, a bear-like hug. I could feel his warm hand grip mine.

It took me back.

Back to the time he held one hand as I pushed my wheelchair along the sidewalk with the other. We were walking home from the local bakery, having just picked out chocolate rugelauch, one of my favorite desserts.

He was smiling, and he listened as I told him that—*someday*—I wanted to write a book about my life. He was a man who accomplished things. As a man of action, he never wasted words about things he wanted to do but hadn't.

"Susan," he said, his blue eyes twinkling. "So write this book already!"

Here then, my father, is my story for you.

EPILOGUE

My mom died the day after I completed this book. She died holding my hand in our living room, surrounded by me, Tom, my friend Cindy and our black and white Newfoundland, Shlomo. Our friend Jenny, who is a physician and guided my mom's palliative care, was also with us.

We were having a conversation by the fireplace and it was as though my mom looked around and thought "everyone who loves Susie is here. This is the time for me to go." There was no coughing, no struggle, no fight. Jenny noticed it was quiet. It seemed my mom died between breaths.

As with some of my other life changing events, I chose a different path. We hugged and kissed my mom as we felt her spirit circle the room. Realizing there was no rush, Tom and I wheeled her to the cabin and did our usual rituals of singing to her and tucking her in bed. I slept by her that night.

The next morning I called the rabbi and close friends and the beautiful Jewish traditions gave me the path to make the necessary funeral arrangements. As I did with my father, I sat shiva for seven days surrounded by friends and family.

Jenny wrote on my mom's death certificate that she died of Genug Syndrome. Genug is a term that translates from Yiddish as "enough already". My close friends and I decided that was the most appropriate term. It was her choice, it was her time.

I still sometimes have chocolate cake for breakfast.

I have no ordinary days.

ABOUT THE AUTHORS

Susan Sygall is a passionate international disability rights activist, wheelchair rider, author, and lecturer. She is the CEO and co-founder of Mobility International USA, an organization that works to advance disability rights and leadership of people with disabilities globally. She has received numerous awards and distinctions in recognition of her work, including the prestigious MacArthur Fellowship, an Ashoka Fellowship, a Rotary Scholarship Alumni Award, Jewish Women International's Women to Watch Award, Kellogg's Matusak Courageous Leadership Award, the "President's Award" from the Honorable Bill Clinton and an honorary doctorate from Chapman University. She lives in Eugene, Oregon with her partner, Tom, and their dog, Yumyum.

Ken Spillman is the author of more than 40 books and the editor of many others. His work spans several genres but he is now best known for his writing for young people. He is a popular international speaker on books, writing and creativity, and has presented sessions to tens of thousands of school children in Australia, China, India, Indonesia, Malaysia, Oman, Philippines and Singapore. For more information, visit www.kenspillman.com.

55596765R00166

Made in the USA
San Bernardino, CA
04 November 2017